Common Core Lessons

Text-Based Writing Nonfiction

Grade 4

Editorial Development: Renee Biermann
Cindie Farley
Lisa Vitarisi Mathews
Copy Editing: Cathy Harber
Art Direction: Cheryl Puckett
Art Management: Kathy Kopp
Cover Design: Yuki Meyer
Cover Illustration: Chris Vallo
Design/Production: Susan Lovell
Jessica Onken

EMC 6034

Evan-Moor®
Helping Children Learn

Visit
teaching-standards.com
to view a correlation
of this book.
This is a free service.

**Correlated to State and
Common Core State Standards**

Contents

What's in Every Unit?

Resource pages outline lesson objectives and provide instructional guidance.

The reading level helps identify appropriate texts.

Lesson objectives and content-area concepts are indicated.

Common Core State Standards correlations are located in each unit for easy reference.

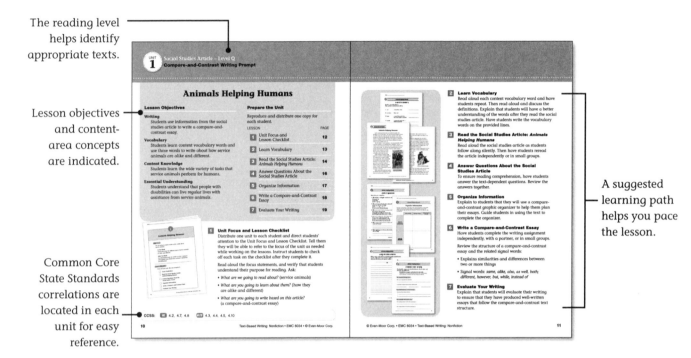

A suggested learning path helps you pace the lesson.

For the Student

Student pages provide unit focus, organizational tools, nonfiction content, and skills practice.

1 Unit Focus and Lesson Checklist

The Unit Focus provides a purpose for reading.

The Lesson Checklist guides students through the learning path.

2 Vocabulary

A dictionary introduces content words and provides definitions.

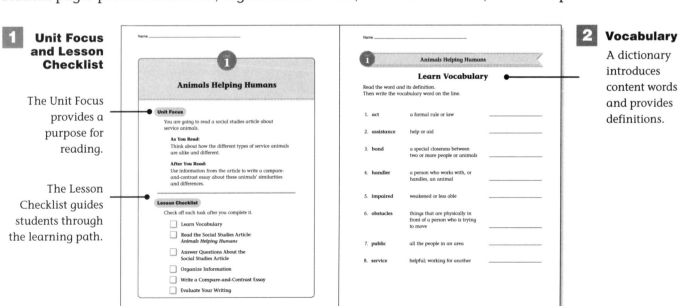

3 Nonfiction Article

A two-page article introduces a content-area topic and provides details.

Illustrations and graphics provide additional information and context.

Animals Helping Humans

Service animals provide safety and stability for people with disabilities. In the United States, the Americans with Disabilities Service Act (ADA) protects the people who use these animals. By law, these animals are allowed into any privately owned business that provides services to the general public. This means the animals are allowed into restaurants, libraries, and even movie theaters. Wherever the person needs to go, the animal can go, too.

The ADA defines a service animal as "any dog individually trained to provide assistance to an individual with a disability." Dogs are common service animals because they can be easily trained to perform a wide variety of tasks. The ADA also lists miniature horses as service animals. Monkeys and certain types of birds are called assistance animals. These animals are not pets. They work hard to help their owners, or handlers, and to keep them safe.

Guide animals are trained to help people who are blind or visually impaired. The animal's job is to help its handler move around safely. These animals help their handlers move through crowded buildings or cross busy streets. They can open doors or alert their handlers to obstacles, such as overhangs or parking meters. The guide animal must pay attention to what is happening all around its handler at all times.

Guide animals also help their handlers use different forms of transportation. Guide horses are small enough to ride in buses

A guide horse helping its visually impaired handler.

and in some cars with their handlers. These animals often wear special shoes for walking on surfaces that might cause them to lose their balance or hurt their feet.

Hearing animals are trained to help people who are deaf or hearing impaired. These animals can tell the difference between a telephone ringing and a smoke alarm going off. They also recognize emergency sirens or knocks on doors. A hearing animal can even be trained to listen for its handler's name. The animal alerts the handler when it hears these sounds by gently pawing or nudging him or her. Then the animal will lead its handler to the sound.

Other general service animals are trained to help people who have a disability that is not related to sight or sound. For example, people who cannot walk or use their arms or hands use service animals to help them walk steadily or to pull their wheelchair. A service dog can pick up things its handler has dropped. In public places, a service dog is trained to bark if its handler needs help. The dog will find someone to help, and then lead that person to the handler.

Some service animals are called "laptop dogs." Laptop dogs must be small and able to jump up onto counters. The dog will retrieve what the handler needs, and then jump with the item onto its handler's lap. Many animals that provide assistance spend most of their lives with their handlers. They not only provide companionship, but they also help their handlers live better lives. The special bond between animal and handler is like no other.

A service dog with its handler.

4 Comprehension Questions

Text-based questions appear in multiple-choice and constructed-response formats.

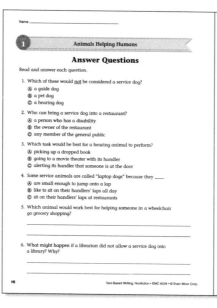

Name _____

Animals Helping Humans

Answer Questions

Read and answer each question.

1. Which of these would not be considered a service dog?
   Ⓐ a guide dog
   Ⓑ a pet dog
   Ⓒ a hearing dog

2. Who can bring a service dog into a restaurant?
   Ⓐ a person who has a disability
   Ⓑ the owner of the restaurant
   Ⓒ any member of the general public

3. Which task would be best for a hearing animal to perform?
   Ⓐ picking up a dropped book
   Ⓑ going to a movie theater with its handler
   Ⓒ alerting its handler that someone is at the door

4. Some service animals are called "laptop dogs" because they ____.
   Ⓐ are small enough to jump onto a lap
   Ⓑ like to sit on their handlers' laps all day
   Ⓒ sit on their handlers' laps at restaurants

5. Which animal would work best for helping someone in a wheelchair go grocery shopping?
   _____

6. What might happen if a librarian did not allow a service dog into a library? Why?
   _____

5 Graphic Organizer

A graphic organizer helps students organize information from the article to plan their writing.

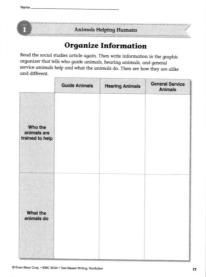

Name _____

Animals Helping Humans

Organize Information

Read the social studies article again. Then write information in the graphic organizer that tells who guide animals, hearing animals, and general service animals help and what the animals do. Then see how they are alike and different.

	Guide Animals	Hearing Animals	General Service Animals
Who the animals are trained to help			
What the animals do			

6 Writing Prompt

A text-based writing prompt helps students synthesize what they've learned.

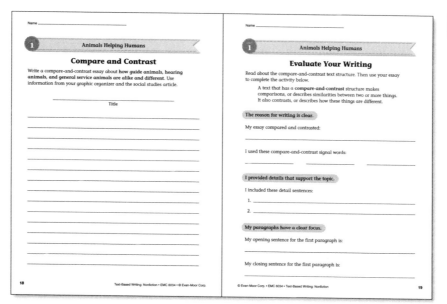

Name _____

Animals Helping Humans

Compare and Contrast

Write a compare-and-contrast essay about how guide animals, hearing animals, and general service animals are alike and different. Use information from your graphic organizer and the social studies article.

_____ Title _____

_____

7 Writing Evaluation

A review of nonfiction writing structures guides students in evaluating their essay.

Name _____

Animals Helping Humans

Evaluate Your Writing

Read about the compare-and-contrast text structure. Then use your essay to complete the activity below.

A text that has a **compare-and-contrast** structure makes comparisons, or describes similarities between two or more things. It also contrasts, or describes how these things are different.

The reason for writing is clear.

My essay compared and contrasted:
_____

I used these compare-and-contrast signal words:
_____

I provided details that support the topic.

I included these detail sentences:
1. _____
2. _____

My paragraphs have a clear focus.

My opening sentence for the first paragraph is:
_____

My closing sentence for the first paragraph is:
_____

Correlations:
Common Core State Standards

	Units					
	1	2	3	4	5	6
W Writing Standards for Grade 4	Animals Helping Humans	The Thirteen Colonies	The Chocolate Process	The Wright Brothers	Peanuts, Please!	California's Big Shakes
Text Types and Purposes						
4.1 Write opinion pieces on topics or texts, supporting a point of view with reasons and information. **a.** Introduce a topic or text clearly, state an opinion, and create an organizational structure in which related ideas are grouped to support the writer's purpose. **b.** Provide reasons that are supported by facts and details.						
4.2 Write informative/explanatory texts to examine a topic and convey ideas and information clearly.	●	●	●	●	●	●
Research to Build and Present Knowledge						
4.7 Conduct short research projects that build knowledge through investigation of different aspects of a topic.	●	●	●	●	●	●
4.8 Recall relevant information from experiences or gather relevant information from print and digital sources; take notes and categorize information, and provide a list of sources.	●	●	●	●	●	●
RIT Reading Standards for Informational Text, Grade 4						
Key Ideas and Details						
4.3 Explain events, procedures, ideas, or concepts in a historical, scientific, or technical text, including what happened and why, based on specific information in the text.	●	●	●	●	●	●
Craft and Structure						
4.4 Determine the meaning of general academic and domain-specific words or phrases in a text relevant to a *grade 4 topic or subject area*.	●	●	●	●	●	●
4.5 Describe the overall structure (e.g., chronology, comparison, cause/effect, problem/solution) of events, ideas, concepts, or information in a text or part of a text.	●	●	●	●	●	●
Range of Reading and Level of Text Complexity						
4.10 By the end of year, read and comprehend informational texts, including history/social studies, science, and technical texts, in the grades 4–5 text complexity band proficiently, with scaffolding as needed at the high end of the range.	●	●	●	●	●	●

Text-Based Writing: Nonfiction • EMC 6034 • © Evan-Moor Corp.

Units						
7	8	9	10	11	12	
Benjamin Franklin	The Biggest Bridge	Genetic Traits	Seeing with Sounds	The Study of Garbage	McDonald Observatory	**W** Writing Standards for Grade 4

Text Types and Purposes

●	●	●	●	●	●	**4.1** Write opinion pieces on topics or texts, supporting a point of view with reasons and information. **a.** Introduce a topic or text clearly, state an opinion, and create an organizational structure in which related ideas are grouped to support the writer's purpose. **b.** Provide reasons that are supported by facts and details.
						4.2 Write informative/explanatory texts to examine a topic and convey ideas and information clearly.

Research to Build and Present Knowledge

●	●	●	●	●	●	**4.7** Conduct short research projects that build knowledge through investigation of different aspects of a topic.
●	●	●	●	●	●	**4.8** Recall relevant information from experiences or gather relevant information from print and digital sources; take notes and categorize information, and provide a list of sources.

RIT Reading Standards for Informational Text, Grade 4

Key Ideas and Details

●	●	●	●	●	●	**4.3** Explain events, procedures, ideas, or concepts in a historical, scientific, or technical text, including what happened and why, based on specific information in the text.

Craft and Structure

●	●	●	●	●	●	**4.4** Determine the meaning of general academic and domain-specific words or phrases in a text relevant to a *grade 4 topic or subject area.*
●	●	●	●	●	●	**4.5** Describe the overall structure (e.g., chronology, comparison, cause/effect, problem/solution) of events, ideas, concepts, or information in a text or part of a text.

Range of Reading and Level of Text Complexity

●	●	●	●	●	●	**4.10** By the end of year, read and comprehend informational texts, including history/social studies, science, and technical texts, in the grades 4–5 text complexity band proficiently, with scaffolding as needed at the high end of the range.

Correlations:
Texas Essential Knowledge and Skills

110.15 English Language Arts and Reading, Grade 4	Units				
	1	2	3	4	5
	Animals Helping Humans	The Thirteen Colonies	The Chocolate Process	The Wright Brothers	Peanuts, Please!
Writing					
(15) Writing/Writing Process. Students use elements of the writing process (planning, drafting, revising, editing, and publishing) to compose text. Students are expected to:	●	●	●	●	●
(A) plan a first draft by selecting ideas and a genre appropriate for conveying the intended meaning to an audience and generating ideas through a range of strategies (e.g., brainstorming, graphic organizers, logs, journals).	●	●	●	●	●
(18) Writing/Expository and Procedural Texts. Students write expository and procedural or work-related texts to communicate ideas and information to specific audiences for specific purposes. Students are expected to:	●	●	●	●	●
(C) write responses to literary or expository texts and provide evidence from the text to demonstrate understanding.	●	●	●	●	●
(19) Writing/Persuasive Texts. Students write persuasive texts to influence the attitudes or actions of a specific audience on specific issues. Students are expected to write persuasive essays for appropriate audiences that establish a position and use supporting details.					
Reading					
(11) Reading/Comprehension of Informational Text/ Expository Text. Students analyze, make inferences, and draw conclusions about expository text and provide evidence from text to support their understanding. Students are expected to:	●	●	●	●	●
(B) distinguish fact from opinion in a text and explain how to verify what is a fact;	●	●	●	●	●
(C) describe explicit and implicit relationships among ideas in texts organized by cause-and-effect, sequence, or comparison; and	●	●	●	●	
(D) use multiple text features (e.g., guide words, topic and concluding sentences) to gain an overview of the contents of text and to locate information.	●	●	●	●	●
(15) Reading/Comprehension of Informational Text/ Procedural Texts. Students understand how to glean and use information in procedural texts and documents. Students are expected to:			●	●	
(A) determine the sequence of activities needed to carry out a procedure (e.g., following a recipe); and			●	●	
(B) use common graphic features to assist in the interpretation of text (e.g., captions, illustrations).	●	●	●	●	●

Units						
6	7	8	9	10	11	12
California's Big Shakes	Benjamin Franklin	The Biggest Bridge	Genetic Traits	Seeing with Sounds	The Study of Garbage	McDonald Observatory
•	•	•	•	•	•	•
•	•	•	•	•	•	•
•						
•	•	•	•	•	•	•
	•	•	•	•	•	•
•	•	•	•	•	•	•
•	•	•	•	•	•	•
•	•		•	•	•	
•	•	•	•	•	•	•
				•		
				•		
•	•	•	•	•	•	•

Animals Helping Humans

Lesson Objectives

Writing
Students use information from the social studies article to write a compare-and-contrast essay.

Vocabulary
Students learn content vocabulary words and use those words to write about how service animals are alike and different.

Content Knowledge
Students learn the wide variety of tasks that service animals perform for humans.

Essential Understanding
Students understand that people with disabilities can live regular lives with assistance from service animals.

Prepare the Unit

Reproduce and distribute one copy for each student.

Name _____

1
Animals Helping Humans

Unit Focus
You are going to read a social studies article about service animals.

As You Read:
Think about how the different types of service animals are alike and different.

After You Read:
Use information from the article to write a compare-and-contrast essay about these animals' similarities and differences.

Lesson Checklist
Check off each task after you complete it.
☐ Learn Vocabulary
☐ Read the Social Studies Article: *Animals Helping Humans*
☐ Answer Questions About the Social Studies Article
☐ Organize Information
☐ Write a Compare-and-Contrast Essay
☐ Evaluate Your Writing

Text-Based Writing: Nonfiction • EMC 6034 • © Evan-Moor Corp.

12

1 **Unit Focus and Lesson Checklist**

Distribute one unit to each student and direct students' attention to the Unit Focus and Lesson Checklist. Tell them they will be able to refer to the focus of the unit as needed while working on the lessons. Instruct students to check off each task on the checklist after they complete it.

Read aloud the focus statements, and verify that students understand their purpose for reading. Ask:

• *What are we going to read about?* (service animals)

• *What are you going to learn about them?* (how they are alike and different)

• *What are you going to write based on this article?* (a compare-and-contrast essay)

CCSS: **W** 4.2, 4.7, 4.8   **RIT** 4.3, 4.4, 4.5, 4.10

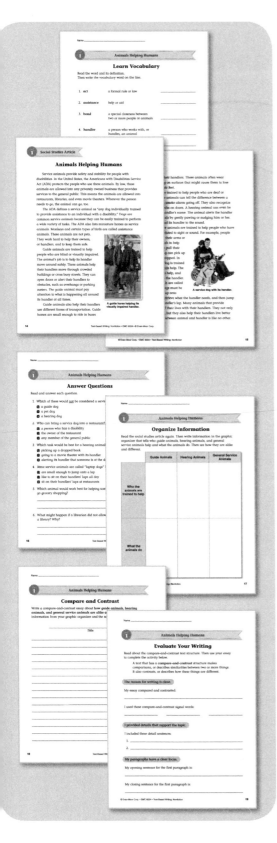

2 Learn Vocabulary

Read aloud each content vocabulary word and have students repeat. Then read aloud and discuss the definitions. Explain that students will have a better understanding of the words after they read the social studies article. Have students write the vocabulary words on the provided lines.

3 Read the Social Studies Article: *Animals Helping Humans*

Read aloud the social studies article as students follow along silently. Then have students reread the article independently or in small groups.

4 Answer Questions About the Social Studies Article

To ensure reading comprehension, have students answer the text-dependent questions. Review the answers together.

5 Organize Information

Explain to students that they will use a compare-and-contrast graphic organizer to help them plan their essays. Guide students in using the text to complete the organizer.

6 Write a Compare-and-Contrast Essay

Have students complete the writing assignment independently, with a partner, or in small groups.

Review the structure of a compare-and-contrast essay and the related signal words:

- Explains similarities and differences between two or more things

- Signal words: *same, alike, also, as well, both; different, however, but, while, instead of*

7 Evaluate Your Writing

Explain that students will evaluate their writing to ensure that they have produced well-written essays that follow the compare-and-contrast text structure.

UNIT
1

Animals Helping Humans

Unit Focus

You are going to read a social studies article about service animals.

As You Read:

Think about how the different types of service animals are alike and different.

After You Read:

Use information from the article to write a compare-and-contrast essay about these animals' similarities and differences.

Lesson Checklist

Check off each task after you complete it.

☐ **Learn Vocabulary**

☐ **Read the Social Studies Article:** *Animals Helping Humans*

☐ **Answer Questions About the Social Studies Article**

☐ **Organize Information**

☐ **Write a Compare-and-Contrast Essay**

☐ **Evaluate Your Writing**

Learn Vocabulary

Read the word and its definition.
Then write the vocabulary word on the line.

1. **act** a formal rule or law _____

2. **assistance** help or aid _____

3. **bond** a special closeness between two or more people or animals _____

4. **handler** a person who works with, or handles, an animal _____

5. **impaired** weakened or less able _____

6. **obstacles** things that are physically in front of a person who is trying to move _____

7. **public** all the people in an area _____

8. **service** helpful; working for another _____

Animals Helping Humans

Service animals provide safety and stability for people with disabilities. In the United States, the Americans with Disabilities Service Act (ADA) protects the people who use these animals. By law, these animals are allowed into any privately owned business that provides services to the general public. This means the animals are allowed into restaurants, libraries, and even movie theaters. Wherever the person needs to go, the animal can go, too.

The ADA defines a service animal as "any dog individually trained to provide assistance to an individual with a disability." Dogs are common service animals because they can be easily trained to perform a wide variety of tasks. The ADA also lists miniature horses as service animals. Monkeys and certain types of birds are called assistance animals. These animals are not pets. They work hard to help their owners, or handlers, and to keep them safe.

A guide horse helping its visually impaired handler.

Guide animals are trained to help people who are blind or visually impaired. The animal's job is to help its handler move around safely. These animals help their handlers move through crowded buildings or cross busy streets. They can open doors or alert their handlers to obstacles, such as overhangs or parking meters. The guide animal must pay attention to what is happening all around its handler at all times.

Guide animals also help their handlers use different forms of transportation. Guide horses are small enough to ride in buses and in some cars with their handlers. These animals often wear special shoes for walking on surfaces that might cause them to lose their balance or hurt their feet.

Hearing animals are trained to help people who are deaf or hearing impaired. These animals can tell the difference between a telephone ringing and a smoke alarm going off. They also recognize emergency sirens or knocks on doors. A hearing animal can even be trained to listen for its handler's name. The animal alerts the handler when it hears these sounds by gently pawing or nudging him or her. Then the animal will lead its handler to the sound.

Other general service animals are trained to help people who have a disability that is not related to sight or sound. For example, people who cannot walk or use their arms or hands use service animals to help them walk steadily or to pull their wheelchair. A service dog can pick up things its handler has dropped. In public places, a service dog is trained to bark if its handler needs help. The dog will find someone to help, and then lead that person to the handler.

A service dog with its handler.

Some service animals are called "laptop dogs." Laptop dogs must be small and able to jump up onto counters. The dog will retrieve what the handler needs, and then jump with the item onto its handler's lap. Many animals that provide assistance spend most of their lives with their handlers. They not only provide companionship, but they also help their handlers live better lives. The special bond between animal and handler is like no other.

Name _____

Answer Questions

Read and answer each question.

1. Which of these would <u>not</u> be considered a service dog?

    Ⓐ a guide dog

    Ⓑ a pet dog

    Ⓒ a hearing dog

2. Who can bring a service dog into a restaurant?

    Ⓐ a person who has a disability

    Ⓑ the owner of the restaurant

    Ⓒ any member of the general public

3. Which task would be best for a hearing animal to perform?

    Ⓐ picking up a dropped book

    Ⓑ going to a movie theater with its handler

    Ⓒ alerting its handler that someone is at the door

4. Some service animals are called "laptop dogs" because they ____.

    Ⓐ are small enough to jump onto a lap

    Ⓑ like to sit on their handlers' laps all day

    Ⓒ sit on their handlers' laps at restaurants

5. Which animal would work best for helping someone in a wheelchair go grocery shopping?

    _____

    _____

6. What might happen if a librarian did not allow a service dog into a library? Why?

    _____

    _____

Text-Based Writing: Nonfiction • EMC 6034 • © Evan-Moor Corp.

Animals Helping Humans

Organize Information

Read the social studies article again. Then write information in the graphic organizer that tells who guide animals, hearing animals, and general service animals help and what the animals do. Then see how they are alike and different.

	Guide Animals	Hearing Animals	General Service Animals
Who the animals are trained to help			
What the animals do			

Compare and Contrast

Write a compare-and-contrast essay about **how guide animals, hearing animals, and general service animals are alike and different**. Use information from your graphic organizer and the social studies article.

_____

Title

_____

_____

_____

_____

_____

_____

_____

_____

_____

_____

_____

_____

_____

UNIT 1

Evaluate Your Writing

Read about the compare-and-contrast text structure. Then use your essay to complete the activity below.

> A text that has a **compare-and-contrast** structure makes comparisons, or describes similarities between two or more things. It also contrasts, or describes how these things are different.

The reason for writing is clear.

My essay compared and contrasted:

_____

I used these compare-and-contrast signal words:

_____   _____   _____

I provided details that support the topic.

I included these detail sentences:

1. _____

2. _____

My paragraphs have a clear focus.

My opening sentence for the first paragraph is:

_____

My closing sentence for the first paragraph is:

_____

The Thirteen Colonies

Lesson Objectives

Writing
Students use information from the social studies article to write a compare-and-contrast essay.

Vocabulary
Students learn content vocabulary words and use those words to write about how the three sets of colonies were alike and different.

Content Knowledge
Students learn about the geography, farming, weather, and people of the colonies.

Essential Understanding
Students understand that the colonists worked very hard to create the United States of America.

Prepare the Unit

Reproduce and distribute one copy for each student.

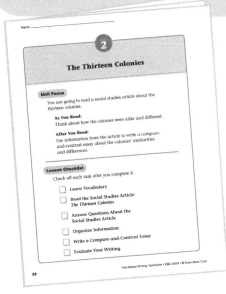

1 **Unit Focus and Lesson Checklist**

Distribute one unit to each student and direct students' attention to the Unit Focus and Lesson Checklist. Tell them they will be able to refer to the focus of the unit as needed while working on the lessons. Instruct students to check off each task on the checklist after they complete it.

Read aloud the focus statements, and verify that students understand their purpose for reading. Ask:

• *What are we going to read about?* (the thirteen colonies)

• *What are you going to learn about them?* (how they were alike and different)

• *What are you going to write based on this article?* (a compare-and-contrast essay)

CCSS: **W** 4.2, 4.7, 4.8 **RIT** 4.3, 4.4, 4.5, 4.10

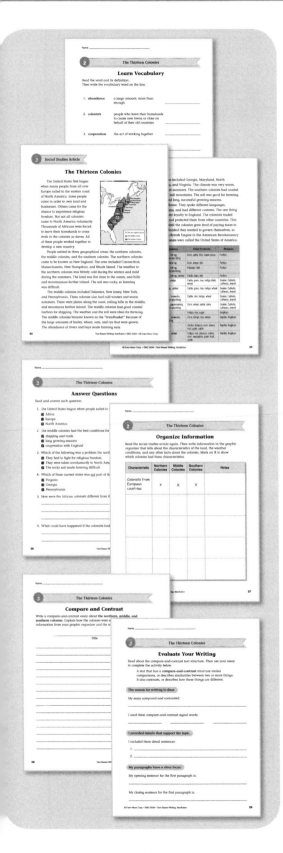

2 Learn Vocabulary

Read aloud each content vocabulary word and have students repeat. Then read aloud and discuss the definitions. Explain that students will have a better understanding of the words after they read the social studies article. Have students write the vocabulary words on the provided lines.

3 Read the Social Studies Article: *The Thirteen Colonies*

Read aloud the social studies article as students follow along silently. Then have students reread the article independently or in small groups.

4 Answer Questions About the Social Studies Article

To ensure reading comprehension, have students answer the text-dependent questions. Review the answers together.

5 Organize Information

Explain to students that they will use a compare-and-contrast graphic organizer to help them plan their essays. Guide students in using the text to complete the organizer.

6 Write a Compare-and-Contrast Essay

Have students complete the writing assignment independently, with a partner, or in small groups.

Review the structure of a compare-and-contrast essay and the related signal words:

• Explains similarities and differences between two or more things

• Signal words: *same, alike, also, as well, both; different, however, but, while, instead of*

7 Evaluate Your Writing

Explain that students will evaluate their writing to ensure that they have produced well-written essays that follow the compare-and-contrast text structure.

UNIT 2

The Thirteen Colonies

Unit Focus

You are going to read a social studies article about the thirteen colonies.

As You Read:

Think about how the colonies were alike and different.

After You Read:

Use information from the article to write a compare-and-contrast essay about the colonies' similarities and differences.

Lesson Checklist

Check off each task after you complete it.

☐ **Learn Vocabulary**

☐ **Read the Social Studies Article:**
The Thirteen Colonies

☐ **Answer Questions About the Social Studies Article**

☐ **Organize Information**

☐ **Write a Compare-and-Contrast Essay**

☐ **Evaluate Your Writing**

The Thirteen Colonies

Learn Vocabulary

Read the word and its definition.
Then write the vocabulary word on the line.

1. **abundance**   a large amount; more than
enough   _____

2. **colonists**   people who leave their homelands
to create new towns or cities on
behalf of their old countries   _____

3. **cooperation**   the act of working together   _____

4. **geographical**   relating to the natural shape or
features of landmasses   _____

5. **harbors**   areas along waterfronts where
ships load and unload goods   _____

6. **ideal**   the best possible or perfect
condition   _____

7. **religious**   relating to religion, or a faith or
belief in a god or gods   _____

8. **voluntarily**   of one's own free will; on purpose   _____

The Thirteen Colonies

The United States first began when many people from all over Europe sailed to the eastern coast of North America. Some people came in order to own land and businesses. Others came for the chance to experience religious freedom. But not all colonists came to North America voluntarily. Thousands of Africans were forced to leave their homelands to come work in the colonies as slaves. All of these people worked together to develop a new country.

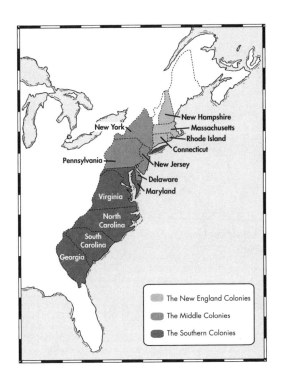

People settled in three geographical areas: the northern colonies, the middle colonies, and the southern colonies. The northern colonies came to be known as New England. The area included Connecticut, Massachusetts, New Hampshire, and Rhode Island. The weather in the northern colonies was bitterly cold during the winters and mild during the summers. The land was flat close to the ocean, and hilly and mountainous farther inland. The soil was rocky, so farming was difficult.

The middle colonies included Delaware, New Jersey, New York, and Pennsylvania. These colonies also had cold winters and warm summers. There were plains along the coast, rolling hills in the middle, and mountains farther inland. The middle colonies had good coastal harbors for shipping. The weather and the soil were ideal for farming. The middle colonies became known as the "breadbasket" because of the large amounts of barley, wheat, oats, and rye that were grown. The abundance of rivers and bays made farming easy.

The southern colonies included Georgia, Maryland, North Carolina, South Carolina, and Virginia. The climate was very warm, with mild winters and hot summers. The southern colonies had coastal plains, rolling hills, and tall mountains. The soil was good for farming, and the weather produced long, successful growing seasons.

Each colony was different. They spoke different languages, practiced different religions, and had different customs. The one thing that united them was their loyalty to England. The colonists traded with England, and England protected them from other countries. This cooperation continued until the colonies grew tired of paying taxes to England. The colonists decided they wanted to govern themselves, so they united to defeat the British Empire in the American Revolutionary War. By 1776, the 13 colonies were called the United States of America.

Colony (year founded)	Economy	Chief Products	Religion
Massachusetts (1620)	Farming, fishing, lumber, shipbuilding	Corn, cattle, fish, maple syrup	Puritan
Connecticut (1633)	Fishing, farming	Corn, wheat, fish	Puritan
New Hampshire (1622)	Farming, fishing, textiles, shipbuilding	Potatoes, fish	Puritan
Rhode Island (1636)	Farming, fishing, lumber	Cattle, dairy, fish	Puritan
Delaware (1638)	Fishing, lumber	Cattle, grain, rice, indigo (dye), wheat	Quaker, Catholic, Lutheran, Jewish
New Jersey (1664)	Ironworks, lumber	Cattle, grain, rice, indigo, wheat	Quaker, Catholic, Lutheran, Jewish
New York (1624)	Farming, ironworks, textiles, shipbuilding	Cattle, rice, indigo, wheat	Quaker, Catholic, Lutheran, Jewish
Pennsylvania (1682)	Farming, papermaking, textiles, shipbuilding	Corn, wheat, cattle, dairy	Quaker, Catholic, Lutheran, Jewish
Georgia (1732)	Farming	Indigo, rice, sugar	Anglican
Maryland (1632)	Farming, ironworks, shipbuilding	Corn, indigo, rice, wheat	Baptist, Anglican
Virginia (1607)	Farming	Cotton, tobacco, corn, wheat, fruit, grain, cattle	Baptist, Anglican
Carolina (1663); North Carolina (1712); South Carolina (1712)	Farming, lumber	Indigo, rice, tobacco, cotton, corn, vegetables, grain, fruit, cattle	Baptist, Anglican

Name _____

Answer Questions

Read and answer each question.

1. The United States began when people sailed to the eastern coast of ____.

   Ⓐ Africa

   Ⓑ Europe

   Ⓒ North America

2. The middle colonies had the best conditions for ____.

   Ⓐ shipping and trade

   Ⓑ long growing seasons

   Ⓒ cooperation with England

3. Which of the following was a problem the northern colonies had?

   Ⓐ They had to fight for religious freedom.

   Ⓑ They were taken involuntarily to North America.

   Ⓒ The rocky soil made farming difficult.

4. Which of these current states was <u>not</u> part of the southern colonies?

   Ⓐ Virginia

   Ⓑ Georgia

   Ⓒ Pennsylvania

5. How were the African colonists different from the rest of the people? Why?

   _____

   _____

   _____

6. What could have happened if the colonists had <u>not</u> rebelled?

   _____

   _____

Organize Information

Read the social studies article again. Then write information in the graphic organizer that tells about the characteristics of the land, the weather conditions, and any other facts about the colonies. Mark an **X** to show which colonies had these characteristics.

Characteristic	Northern Colonies	Middle Colonies	Southern Colonies	Notes
Colonists from European countries	X	X	X	

Name _____

Compare and Contrast

Write a compare-and-contrast essay about **the northern, middle, and southern colonies**. Explain how the colonies were alike and different. Use information from your graphic organizer and the social studies article.

_____
Title

_____

_____

_____

_____

_____

_____

_____

_____

_____

_____

_____

_____

Name _____

Evaluate Your Writing

Read about the compare-and-contrast text structure. Then use your essay to complete the activity below.

> A text that has a **compare-and-contrast** structure makes comparisons, or describes similarities between two or more things. It also contrasts, or describes how these things are different.

The reason for writing is clear.

My essay compared and contrasted:

_____

I used these compare-and-contrast signal words:

_____   _____   _____

I provided details that support the topic.

I included these detail sentences:

1. _____

2. _____

My paragraphs have a clear focus.

My opening sentence for the first paragraph is:

_____

My closing sentence for the first paragraph is:

_____

The Chocolate Process

Lesson Objectives

Writing
Students use information from the science article to write a cause-and-effect essay.

Vocabulary
Students learn content vocabulary words and use those words to write about how growing and eating chocolate helps farmers, workers, shops, and everyday people.

Content Knowledge
Students learn where chocolate comes from and the steps needed to produce various products.

Essential Understanding
Students understand that along with giving people a sweet treat, many jobs are created through the chocolate process.

Prepare the Unit

Reproduce and distribute one copy for each student.

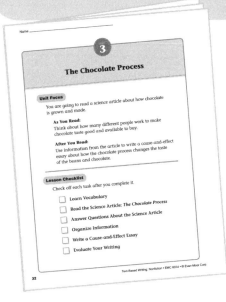

1 Unit Focus and Lesson Checklist

Distribute one unit to each student and direct students' attention to the Unit Focus and Lesson Checklist. Tell them they will be able to refer to the focus of the unit as needed while working on the lessons. Instruct students to check off each task on the checklist after they complete it.

Read aloud the focus statements, and verify that students understand their purpose for reading. Ask:

• *What are we going to read about?* (how chocolate is grown and made)

• *What are you going to learn about?* (the people who make and sell chocolate)

• *What are you going to write based on this science article?* (a cause-and-effect essay)

CCSS: **W** 4.2, 4.7, 4.8   **RIT** 4.3, 4.4, 4.5, 4.10

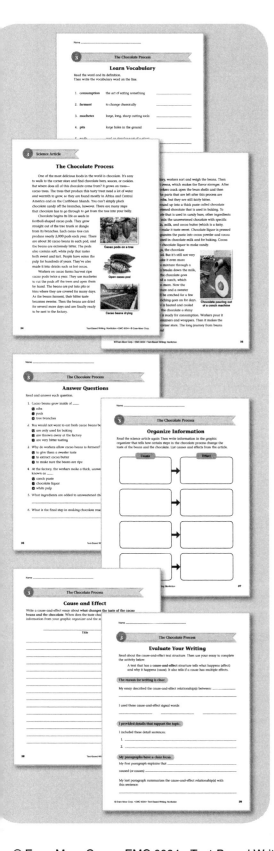

2 Learn Vocabulary

Read aloud each content vocabulary word and have students repeat. Then read aloud and discuss the definitions. Explain that students will have a better understanding of the words after they read the science article. Have students write the vocabulary words on the provided lines.

3 Read the Science Article: *The Chocolate Process*

Read aloud the science article as students follow along silently. Then have students reread the article independently or in small groups.

4 Answer Questions About the Science Article

To ensure reading comprehension, have students answer the text-dependent questions. Review the answers together.

5 Organize Information

Explain to students that they will use a cause-and-effect graphic organizer to help them plan their essays. Guide students in using the text to complete the organizer.

6 Write a Cause-and-Effect Essay

Have students complete the writing assignment independently, with a partner, or in small groups.

Review the structure of a cause-and-effect essay and the related signal words:

• Explains what happened (effect) and why it happened (cause)

• Signal words: *because, therefore, so, since, as a result*

7 Evaluate Your Writing

Explain that students will evaluate their writing to ensure that they have produced well-written essays that follow the cause-and-effect text structure.

The Chocolate Process

Unit Focus

You are going to read a science article about how chocolate is grown and made.

As You Read:

Think about how many different people work to make chocolate taste good and available to buy.

After You Read:

Use information from the article to write a cause-and-effect essay about how the chocolate process changes the taste of the beans and chocolate.

Lesson Checklist

Check off each task after you complete it.

- [ ] **Learn Vocabulary**
- [ ] **Read the Science Article:** *The Chocolate Process*
- [ ] **Answer Questions About the Science Article**
- [ ] **Organize Information**
- [ ] **Write a Cause-and-Effect Essay**
- [ ] **Evaluate Your Writing**

Learn Vocabulary

Read the word and its definition.
Then write the vocabulary word on the line.

1. **consumption**   the act of eating something   _____

2. **ferment**   to change chemically   _____

3. **machetes**   large, long, sharp cutting tools   _____

4. **pits**   large holes in the ground   _____

5. **pods**   oval or circular part of a plant that contains seeds   _____

6. **pulp**   a soft, squishy substance found inside fruit or pods   _____

7. **tart**   sour tasting (such as lemons)   _____

8. **texture**   the way something feels, such as soft, hard, rough, or smooth   _____

The Chocolate Process

One of the most delicious foods in the world is chocolate. It's easy to walk to the corner store and find chocolate bars, sauces, or cookies. But where does all of this chocolate come from? It grows on trees— cacao trees. The trees that produce this tasty treat need a lot of water and warmth to grow, so they are found mostly in Africa and Central America and on the Caribbean Islands. You can't simply pluck chocolate candy off the branches, however. There are many steps that chocolate has to go through to get from the tree into your belly.

Chocolate begins its life as seeds in football-shaped cacao pods. They grow straight out of the tree trunk or dangle from its branches. Each cacao tree can produce nearly 2,000 pods each year. There are about 30 cacao beans in each pod, and the beans are extremely bitter. The pods also contain soft, white pulp that tastes both sweet and tart. People have eaten the pulp for hundreds of years. They've also made it into drinks such as hot cocoa.

Cacao pods on a tree

Open cacao pod

Workers on cacao farms harvest ripe cacao pods twice a year. They use machetes to cut the pods off the trees and open them by hand. The beans are put into pits or bins where they are covered for many days. As the beans ferment, their bitter taste becomes sweeter. Then the beans are dried for several more days and are finally ready to be sent to the factory.

Cacao beans drying

At the chocolate factory, workers sort and weigh the beans. Then they are roasted in giant ovens, which makes the flavor stronger. After roasting is completed, workers crack open the bean shells and then throw the shells away. The parts that are left after this process are called nibs. You can eat nibs, but they are still fairly bitter.

Next, the nibs are ground up into a thick paste called chocolate liquor. This is the unsweetened chocolate that is used in baking. To make the kind of chocolate that is used in candy bars, other ingredients must be added. Workers mix the unsweetened chocolate with specific amounts of sugar, vanilla, milk, and cocoa butter (which is a fatty, yellow, solid material) to make it taste sweet. Chocolate liquor is pressed in a big machine that separates the paste into cocoa powder and cocoa butter. Cocoa powder is used in chocolate milk and for baking. Cocoa butter is added back into chocolate liquor to make candy.

After all of these steps, the chocolate mixture tastes pretty good. But it's still not very smooth or creamy. To make it even more delicious, workers put the mixture through a series of steel rollers. This breaks down the milk, cocoa, and sugar. Then the chocolate goes through a machine called a conch, which blends the chocolate even more. Now the chocolate has a silky texture and a sweeter taste. Most chocolate will be conched for a few hours, but sometimes conching goes on for days.

Chocolate pouring out of a conch machine

Finally, the chocolate is heated and cooled several times. This gives the chocolate a shiny look. Then the chocolate is ready for consumption. Workers pour it into different kinds of containers and wrappers. Then it makes the journey to your favorite corner store. The long journey from beans to bars has been a success!

The Chocolate Process

Answer Questions

Read and answer each question.

1. Cacao beans grow inside of ____.

   Ⓐ nibs

   Ⓑ pods

   Ⓒ tree branches

2. You would not want to eat fresh cacao beans because they ____.

   Ⓐ are only used for baking

   Ⓑ are thrown away at the factory

   Ⓒ are very bitter tasting

3. Why do workers allow cacao beans to ferment?

   Ⓐ to give them a sweeter taste

   Ⓑ to extract cocoa butter

   Ⓒ to make sure the beans are ripe

4. At the factory, the workers make a thick, unsweetened chocolate paste known as ____.

   Ⓐ conch paste

   Ⓑ chocolate liquor

   Ⓒ white pulp

5. What ingredients are added to unsweetened chocolate to make it sweet?

   _____

6. What is the final step in making chocolate ready for consumption?

   _____

Organize Information

Read the science article again Then write information in the graphic organizer that tells how certain steps in the chocolate process change the taste of the beans and the chocolate. List causes and effects from the article.

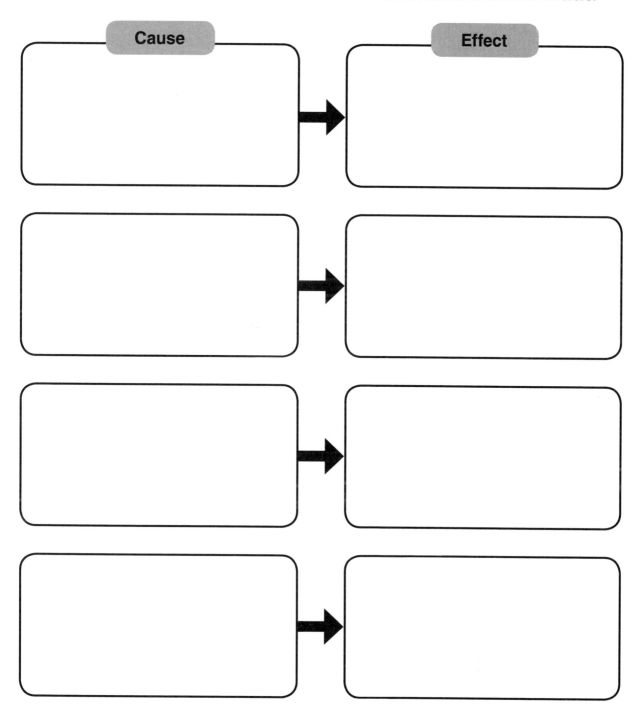

Name _____

Cause and Effect

Write a cause-and-effect essay about **what changes the taste of the cacao beans and the chocolate**. When does the taste change and why? Use information from your graphic organizer and the science article.

_____

Title

_____

_____

_____

_____

_____

_____

_____

_____

_____

_____

_____

_____

Name _____

Evaluate Your Writing

Read about the cause-and-effect text structure. Then use your essay to complete the activity below.

A text that has a **cause-and-effect** structure tells what happens (effect) and why it happens (cause). It also tells if a cause has multiple effects.

The reason for writing is clear.

My essay described the cause-and-effect relationship(s) between: _____

_____

I used these cause-and-effect signal words:

_____   _____   _____

I provided details that support the topic.

I included these detail sentences:

1. _____

2. _____

My paragraphs have a clear focus.

My first paragraph explains that _____

caused (or causes) _____

My last paragraph summarizes the cause-and-effect relationship(s) with this sentence:

_____

The Wright Brothers

Lesson Objectives

Writing
Students use information from the biography to write a cause-and-effect essay.

Vocabulary
Students learn content vocabulary words and use those words to write about how the Wright brothers changed the way people travel.

Content Knowledge
Students learn about the challenges of past travel methods and how they have improved.

Essential Understanding
Students understand that inventors such as the Wright brothers worked to make travel easier and safer for people today.

Prepare the Unit

Reproduce and distribute one copy for each student.

1 Unit Focus and Lesson Checklist

Distribute one unit to each student and direct students' attention to the Unit Focus and Lesson Checklist. Tell them they will be able to refer to the focus of the unit as needed while working on the lessons. Instruct students to check off each task on the checklist after they complete it.

Read aloud the focus statements, and verify that students understand their purpose for reading. Ask:

- *Who are we going to read about?* (Wilbur and Orville Wright)

- *What are you going to learn about them?* (how they changed the way people travel)

- *What are you going to write based on this biography?* (a cause-and-effect essay)

CCSS: **W** 4.2, 4.7, 4.8 **RIT** 4.3, 4.4, 4.5, 4.10

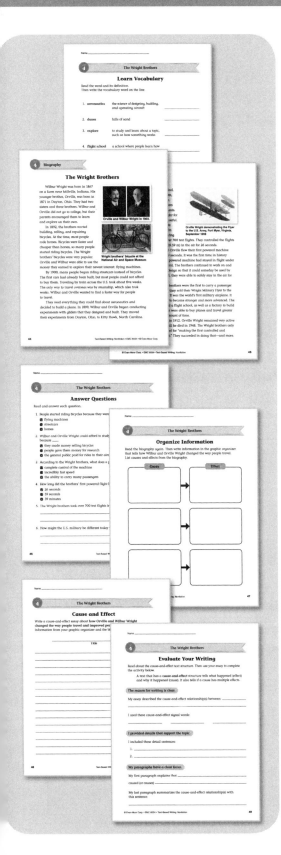

2 Learn Vocabulary

Read aloud each content vocabulary word and have students repeat. Then read aloud and discuss the definitions. Explain that students will have a better understanding of the words after they read the biography. Have students write the vocabulary words on the provided lines.

3 Read the Biography: *The Wright Brothers*

Read aloud the biography as students follow along silently. Then have students reread the biography independently or in small groups.

4 Answer Questions About the Biography

To ensure reading comprehension, have students answer the text-dependent questions. Review the answers together.

5 Organize Information

Explain to students that they will use a cause-and-effect graphic organizer to help them plan their essays. Guide students in using the text to complete the organizer.

6 Write a Cause-and-Effect Essay

Have students complete the writing assignment independently, with a partner, or in small groups.

Review the structure of a cause-and-effect essay and the related signal words:

- Explains what happened (effect) and why it happened (cause)

- Signal words: *because, therefore, so, since, as a result*

7 Evaluate Your Writing

Explain that students will evaluate their writing to ensure that they have produced well-written essays that follow the cause-and-effect text structure.

UNIT
4

The Wright Brothers

Unit Focus

You are going to read a biography about Wilbur and Orville Wright.

As You Read:

Think about how the brothers' inventions changed the way people travel.

After You Read:

Use information from the article to write a cause-and-effect essay about how the Wright brothers changed the way people travel.

Lesson Checklist

Check off each task after you complete it.

- [ ] **Learn Vocabulary**

- [ ] **Read the Biography:** *The Wright Brothers*

- [ ] **Answer Questions About the Biography**

- [ ] **Organize Information**

- [ ] **Write a Cause-and-Effect Essay**

- [ ] **Evaluate Your Writing**

Name _____

Learn Vocabulary

Read the word and its definition.
Then write the vocabulary word on the line.

1. **aeronautics**   the science of designing, building, and operating aircraft   _____

2. **dunes**   hills of sand   _____

3. **explore**   to study and learn about a topic, such as how something works   _____

4. **flight school**   a school where people learn how to properly operate aircraft   _____

5. **flying machine**   a machine that has wings and moves through the air above the ground   _____

6. **gliders**   aircraft that glide, or move, without using an engine   _____

7. **powered machine**   a machine that uses an engine and requires fuel to work   _____

8. **sustained**   lasting over a long period of time   _____

The Wright Brothers

Wilbur Wright was born in 1867 on a farm near Millville, Indiana. His younger brother, Orville, was born in 1871 in Dayton, Ohio. They had two sisters and three brothers. Wilbur and Orville did not go to college, but their parents encouraged them to learn and explore on their own.

Orville and Wilbur Wright in 1903.

In 1892, the brothers started building, selling, and repairing bicycles. At the time, most people rode horses. Bicycles were faster and cheaper than horses, so many people started riding bicycles. The Wright brothers' bicycles were very popular. Orville and Wilbur were able to use the

Wright brothers' bicycle at the National Air and Space Museum

money they earned to explore their newest interest: flying machines.

By 1900, many people began riding streetcars instead of bicycles. The first cars had already been built, but most people could not afford to buy them. Traveling by train across the U.S. took about five weeks. The only way to travel overseas was by steamship, which also took weeks. Wilbur and Orville wanted to find a faster way for people to travel.

They read everything they could find about aeronautics and decided to build a plane. In 1899, Wilbur and Orville began conducting experiments with gliders that they designed and built. They moved their experiments from Dayton, Ohio, to Kitty Hawk, North Carolina.

Kitty Hawk had more wind, tall dunes to take off from, and soft sand to land on. For four years, the brothers continued their experiments. They believed that in order for a flying machine to be useful, the pilot needed complete control of the machine. In 1902, they took turns flying

Orville Wright demonstrating the Flyer to the U.S. Army, Fort Myer, Virginia, September 1908

one of their gliders in over 700 test flights. They controlled the flights and traveled 622 feet (189.59 m) in the air for 26 seconds.

In 1903, Wilbur and Orville flew their first powered machine 852 feet (259.69 m) in 59 seconds. It was the first time in history that a heavier-than-air, powered machine had stayed in flight under the pilot's complete control. The brothers continued to work on and improve the machine's design so that it could someday be used by people to travel. By 1905, they were able to safely stay in the air for 39 minutes.

In 1908, the Wright brothers were the first to carry a passenger in an airplane. In 1909, they sold their Wright Military Flyer to the U.S. Army Signal Corps. It was the world's first military airplane. It helped the U.S. military to become stronger and more advanced. The brothers then established a flight school, as well as a factory to build their planes. Now people were able to buy planes and travel greater distances in a shorter amount of time.

Wilbur Wright died in 1912. Orville Wright remained very active in the world of flight until he died in 1948. The Wright brothers only wanted to be remembered for "making the first controlled and sustained powered flight." They succeeded in doing that—and more.

UNIT
4

The Wright Brothers

Answer Questions

Read and answer each question.

1. People started riding bicycles because they were faster than ____.
   - Ⓐ flying machines
   - Ⓑ streetcars
   - Ⓒ horses

2. Wilbur and Orville Wright could afford to study flying machines because ____.
   - Ⓐ they made money selling bicycles
   - Ⓑ people gave them money for research
   - Ⓒ the general public paid for rides in their aircraft

3. According to the Wright brothers, what does a pilot need to have?
   - Ⓐ complete control of the machine
   - Ⓑ incredibly fast speed
   - Ⓒ the ability to carry many passengers

4. How long did the brothers' first powered flight last?
   - Ⓐ 26 seconds
   - Ⓑ 59 seconds
   - Ⓒ 39 minutes

5. The Wright brothers took over 700 test flights in their glider. Why?

   _____

   _____

6. How might the U.S. military be different today without the Wright brothers?

   _____

   _____

Organize Information

Read the biography again. Then write information in the graphic organizer that tells how Wilbur and Orville Wright changed the way people travel. List causes and effects from the biography.

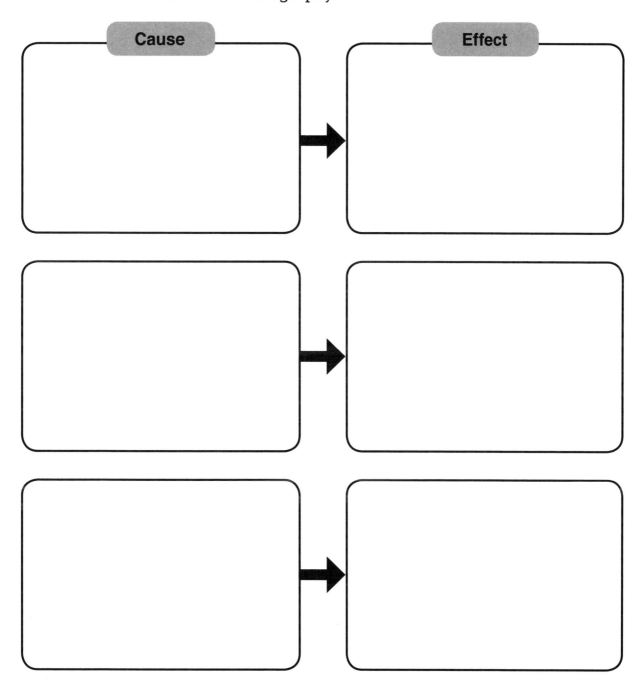

Cause

Effect

Name _____

Cause and Effect

Write a cause-and-effect essay about **how Orville and Wilbur Wright changed the way people travel and improved people's lives.** Use information from your graphic organizer and the biography.

_____

Title

_____

_____

_____

_____

_____

_____

_____

_____

_____

_____

_____

Name _____

Evaluate Your Writing

Read about the cause-and-effect text structure. Then use your essay to complete the activity below.

A text that has a **cause-and-effect** structure tells what happened (effect) and why it happened (cause). It also tells if a cause has multiple effects.

The reason for writing is clear.

My essay described the cause-and-effect relationship(s) between: _____

_____

I used these cause-and-effect signal words:

_____   _____   _____

I provided details that support the topic.

I included these detail sentences:

1. _____

2. _____

My paragraphs have a clear focus.

My first paragraph explains that _____

caused (or causes) _____

My last paragraph summarizes the cause-and-effect relationship(s) with this sentence:

_____

Peanuts, Please!

Lesson Objectives

Writing
Students use information from the social studies article to write an informative essay.

Vocabulary
Students learn content vocabulary words and use those words to write about peanuts in the past and the present.

Content Knowledge
Students understand and can explain that peanuts were and are used as food.

Essential Understanding
Students understand that peanuts and peanut butter provide protein, which is an essential human dietary need.

Prepare the Unit

Reproduce and distribute one copy for each student.

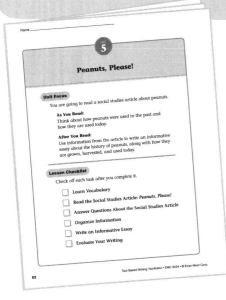

1 Unit Focus and Lesson Checklist

Distribute one unit to each student and direct students' attention to the Unit Focus and Lesson Checklist. Tell them they will be able to refer to the focus of the unit as needed while working on the lessons. Instruct students to check off each task on the checklist after they complete it.

Read aloud the focus statements, and verify that students understand their purpose for reading. Ask:

- *What are we going to read about?* (peanuts)

- *What are you going to learn about them?* (how they were used in the past and how they are used today)

- *What are you going to write based on this article?* (an informative essay)

CCSS: **W** 4.2, 4.7, 4.8 **RIT** 4.3, 4.4, 4.5, 4.10

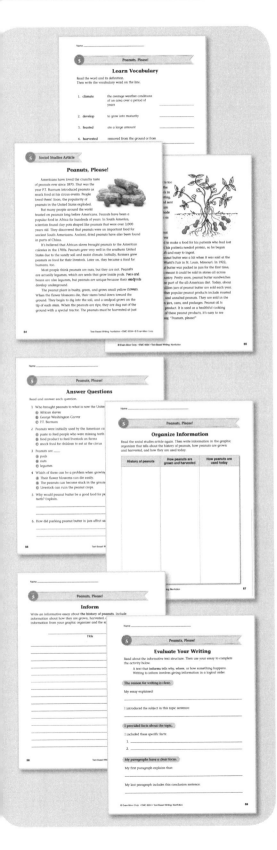

2 ## Learn Vocabulary

Read aloud each content vocabulary word and have students repeat. Then read aloud and discuss the definitions. Explain that students will have a better understanding of the words after they read the social studies article. Have students write the vocabulary words on the provided lines.

3 ## Read the Social Studies Article: *Peanuts, Please!*

Read aloud the social studies article as students follow along silently. Then have students reread the article independently or in small groups.

4 ## Answer Questions About the Social Studies Article

To ensure reading comprehension, have students answer the text-dependent questions. Review the answers together.

5 ## Organize Information

Explain to students that they will use a topic-and-details graphic organizer to help them plan their essays. Guide students in using the text to complete the organizer.

6 ## Write an Informative Essay

Have students complete the writing assignment independently, with a partner, or in small groups.

Review the structure of an informative essay:

- Tells why, where, or how something happens
- Tells information in a logical sequence
- Includes an introductory topic sentence and a conclusion sentence at the end

7 ## Evaluate Your Writing

Explain that students will evaluate their writing to ensure that they have produced well-written essays that follow the informative text structure.

UNIT
5

Peanuts, Please!

Unit Focus

You are going to read a social studies article about peanuts.

As You Read:

Think about how peanuts were used in the past and how they are used today.

After You Read:

Use information from the article to write an informative essay about the history of peanuts, along with how they are grown, harvested, and used today.

Lesson Checklist

Check off each task after you complete it.

☐ **Learn Vocabulary**

☐ **Read the Social Studies Article:** *Peanuts, Please!*

☐ **Answer Questions About the Social Studies Article**

☐ **Organize Information**

☐ **Write an Informative Essay**

☐ **Evaluate Your Writing**

Learn Vocabulary

Read the word and its definition.
Then write the vocabulary word on the line.

1. **climate**   the average weather conditions
                     of an area over a period of
                     years   _____

2. **develop**   to grow into maturity   _____

3. **feasted**   ate a large amount   _____

4. **harvested**   removed from the ground or from
                     plants to be stored or sold   _____

5. **initially**   at the beginning; at first   _____

6. **livestock**   animals that are raised for food
                     or work purposes, such as cows,
                     sheep, goats, or horses   _____

7. **protein**   a substance in the human body
                     that is necessary for the repair
                     and growth of healthy cells   _____

8. **ripe**   fully grown or matured; ready
                     to be eaten   _____

Peanuts, Please!

Americans have loved the crunchy taste of peanuts ever since 1870. That was the year P.T. Barnum introduced peanuts as snack food at his circus events. People loved them! Soon, the popularity of peanuts in the United States exploded.

But many people around the world feasted on peanuts long before Americans. Peanuts have been a popular food in Africa for hundreds of years. In South America, scientists found clay pots shaped like peanuts that were over 3,000 years old. They discovered that peanuts were an important food for ancient South Americans. Ancient, dried peanuts have also been found in parts of China.

It's believed that African slaves brought peanuts to the American colonies in the 1700s. Peanuts grew very well in the southern United States due to the sandy soil and moist climate. Initially, farmers grew peanuts as food for their livestock. Later on, they became a food for humans, too.

Most people think peanuts are nuts, but they are not. Peanuts are actually legumes, which are seeds that grow inside pods. Peas and beans are also legumes, but peanuts are unique because their seedpods develop underground.

The peanut plant is bushy, green, and grows small yellow flowers. When the flower blossoms die, their stems bend down toward the ground. They begin to dig into the soil, and a seedpod grows on the tip of each stem. When the peanuts are ripe, they are dug out of the ground with a special tractor. The peanuts must be harvested at just

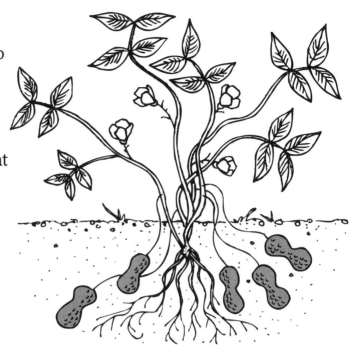

the right time. If the soil is too wet or too dry, many of the peanuts will remain stuck in the ground. After harvesting, the peanuts are dried and sent to factories. There, they are packaged as snacks or made into other products, such as peanut butter.

George Washington Carver developed a peanut butter around 1890. Carver was a doctor who wanted to make a food for his patients who had lost their teeth. He knew that his patients needed protein, so he began looking for something soft and easy to ingest.

Peanut butter was a hit when it was sold at the 1904 World's Fair in St. Louis, Missouri. In 1922, peanut butter was packed in jars for the first time, which meant it could be sold in stores all across the country. Pretty soon, peanut butter sandwiches became part of the all-American diet. Today, about 170 million jars of peanut butter are sold each year.

Other popular peanut products include roasted peanuts, salted peanuts, and unsalted peanuts. They are sold in the shell or out of the shell in jars, cans, and packages. Peanut oil is another popular peanut product. It is used as a healthful cooking oil to fry foods. With all of these peanut products, it's easy to see why people continue to say, "Peanuts, please!"

UNIT 5

Peanuts, Please!

Answer Questions

Read and answer each question.

1. Who brought peanuts to what is now the United States?

   Ⓐ African slaves

   Ⓑ George Washington Carver

   Ⓒ P.T. Barnum

2. Peanuts were initially used by the American colonies as a ____.

   Ⓐ paste to feed people who were missing teeth

   Ⓑ food product to feed livestock on farms

   Ⓒ snack food for children to eat at the circus

3. Peanuts are ____.

   Ⓐ pods

   Ⓑ nuts

   Ⓒ legumes

4. Which of these can be a problem when growing peanuts?

   Ⓐ Their flower blossoms can die easily.

   Ⓑ The peanuts can become stuck in the ground.

   Ⓒ Livestock can ruin the peanut crops.

5. Why would peanut butter be a good food for people who are missing teeth? Explain.

   _____

   _____

6. How did packing peanut butter in jars affect sales?

   _____

   _____

UNIT
5

Peanuts, Please!

Organize Information

Read the social studies article again. Then write information in the graphic organizer that tells about the history of peanuts, how peanuts are grown and harvested, and how they are used today.

History of peanuts	How peanuts are grown and harvested	How peanuts are used today

Inform

Write an informative essay about **the history of peanuts**. Include information about how they are grown, harvested, and used today. Use information from your graphic organizer and the social studies article.

_____

Title

_____

_____

_____

_____

_____

_____

_____

_____

_____

_____

_____

_____

_____

Name _____

Evaluate Your Writing

Read about the informative text structure. Then use your essay to complete the activity below.

A text that **informs** tells why, where, or how something happens. Writing to inform involves giving information in a logical order.

The reason for writing is clear.

My essay explained:

_____

I introduced the subject in this topic sentence:

_____

I provided facts about the topic.

I included these specific facts:

1. _____

2. _____

My paragraphs have a clear focus.

My first paragraph explains that:

_____

My last paragraph includes this conclusion sentence:

_____

California's Big Shakes

Lesson Objectives

Writing
Students use information from the science article to write an explanatory essay.

Vocabulary
Students learn content vocabulary words and use those words to write about the San Andreas Fault and earthquakes.

Content Knowledge
Students learn about the geological causes of earthquakes and the dangers of living in a fault zone.

Essential Understanding
Students understand that earthquakes can have devastating effects on the land and on people.

Prepare the Unit

Reproduce and distribute one copy for each student.

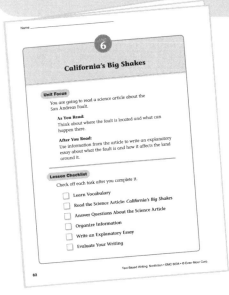

1 **Unit Focus and Lesson Checklist**

Distribute one unit to each student and direct students' attention to the Unit Focus and Lesson Checklist. Tell them they will be able to refer to the focus of the unit as needed while working on the lessons. Instruct students to check off each task on the checklist after they complete it.

Read aloud the focus statements, and verify that students understand their purpose for reading. Ask:

• *What are we going to read about?* (the San Andreas Fault)

• *What are you going to learn about it?* (where it is; what happens there)

• *What are you going to write based on this article?* (an explanatory essay)

CCSS: **W** 4.2, 4.7, 4.8   **RIT** 4.3, 4.4, 4.5, 4.10

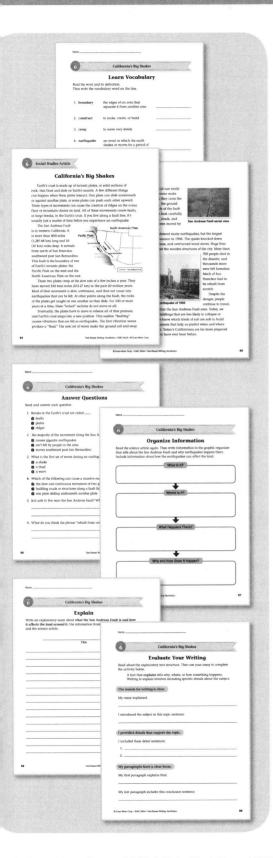

2 Learn Vocabulary

Read aloud each content vocabulary word and have students repeat. Then read aloud and discuss the definitions. Explain that students will have a better understanding of the words after they read the science article. Have students write the vocabulary words on the provided lines.

3 Read the Science Article: *California's Big Shakes*

Read aloud the science article as students follow along silently. Then have students reread the article independently or in small groups.

4 Answer Questions About the Science Article

To ensure reading comprehension, have students answer the text-dependent questions. Review the answers together.

5 Organize Information

Explain to students that they will use a topic-and-details graphic organizer to help them plan their essays. Guide students in using the text to complete the organizer.

6 Write an Explanatory Essay

Have students complete the writing assignment independently, with a partner, or in small groups.

Review the structure of an explanatory essay:

- Tells why, where, or how something happens
- Includes specific details about the topic
- Includes an introductory topic sentence and a conclusion sentence at the end

7 Evaluate Your Writing

Explain that students will evaluate their writing to ensure that they have produced well-written essays that follow the explanatory text structure.

UNIT
6

California's Big Shakes

Unit Focus

You are going to read a science article about the San Andreas Fault.

As You Read:

Think about where the fault is located and what can happen there.

After You Read:

Use information from the article to write an explanatory essay about what the fault is and how it affects the land around it.

Lesson Checklist

Check off each task after you complete it.

- [ ] **Learn Vocabulary**
- [ ] **Read the Science Article: *California's Big Shakes***
- [ ] **Answer Questions About the Science Article**
- [ ] **Organize Information**
- [ ] **Write an Explanatory Essay**
- [ ] **Evaluate Your Writing**

Learn Vocabulary

Read the word and its definition.
Then write the vocabulary word on the line.

1. **boundary**   the edges of an area that separate it from another area   _____

2. **construct**   to make, create, or build   _____

3. **creep**   to move very slowly   _____

4. **earthquake** an event in which the earth shakes or moves for a period of seconds or minutes   _____

5. **from scratch**   from the beginning; without any previous work   _____

6. **interact**   to come in contact with   _____

7. **mantle**   the hot, liquid matter that is located in between the Earth's crust and core   _____

8. **zone**   a certain area of land   _____

California's Big Shakes

Earth's crust is made up of tectonic plates, or solid sections of rock, that float and slide on Earth's mantle. A few different things can happen when these plates interact. One plate can slide underneath or against another plate, or some plates can push each other upward. These types of movements can cause the creation of ridges on the ocean floor or mountain chains on land. All of these movements create faults, or large breaks, in the Earth's crust. If you live along a fault line, it's usually just a matter of time before you experience an earthquake.

The San Andreas Fault is in western California. It is more than 800 miles (1,287.48 km) long and 10 miles (16 km) deep. It extends from north of San Francisco southward past San Bernardino. This fault is the boundary of two of Earth's tectonic plates: the Pacific Plate on the west and the North American Plate on the east.

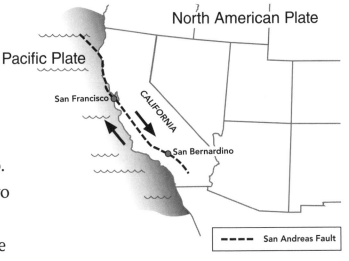

These two plates creep at the slow rate of a few inches a year. They have moved 350 total miles (563.27 km) in the past 20 million years. Most of their movement is slow, continuous, and does not cause any earthquakes that can be felt. At other points along the fault, the rocks of the plates get caught on one another as they slide. For 100 or more years at a time, these "locked" sections do not move at all.

Eventually, the plates have to move to release all of that pressure, and Earth's crust snaps into a new position. This sudden "faulting" causes vibrations that are felt as earthquakes. The first vibration waves produce a "thud." The next set of waves make the ground roll and sway.

The San Andreas Fault can easily be seen from the air. Streams make sudden right turns when they cross the fault line. In some spots, the ground looks different on one side of the fault than on the other. If you look carefully, you can often see fences, roads, and rows of trees that have been moved by earthquakes in the past.

San Andreas Fault aerial view

California has experienced many earthquakes, but the largest one happened in San Francisco in 1906. The quake knocked down buildings, broke power lines, and overturned wood stoves. Huge fires spread quickly throughout the wooden structures of the city. More than 700 people died in the disaster, and thousands more were left homeless. Much of San Francisco had to be rebuilt from scratch.

San Francisco Earthquake of 1906

Despite the danger, people continue to travel, live, and do business within the San Andreas Fault zone. Today, we know how to construct buildings that are less likely to collapse or burn in earthquakes. We know which kinds of soil are safe to build on. We even have instruments that help us predict when and where earthquakes might occur. Today's Californians are far more prepared for "big shakes" than they have ever been before.

Name _____

Answer Questions

Read and answer each question.

1. Breaks in the Earth's crust are called ____.

   Ⓐ faults

   Ⓑ plates

   Ⓒ ridges

2. The majority of the movement along the San Andreas Fault ____.

   Ⓐ causes gigantic earthquakes

   Ⓑ isn't felt by people in the area

   Ⓒ moves southward past San Bernardino

3. What is the first set of waves during an earthquake felt as?

   Ⓐ a shake

   Ⓑ a thud

   Ⓒ a wave

4. Which of the following can cause a massive earthquake?

   Ⓐ the slow and continuous movement of two plates

   Ⓑ building roads or structures along a fault line

   Ⓒ one plate sliding underneath another plate

5. Is it safe to live near the San Andreas Fault? Why or why not?

   _____

   _____

6. What do you think the phrase "rebuilt from scratch" means?

   _____

   _____

Name _____

Organize Information

Read the science article again. Then write information in the graphic organizer that tells about the San Andreas Fault and why earthquakes happen there. Include information about how the earthquakes can affect the land.

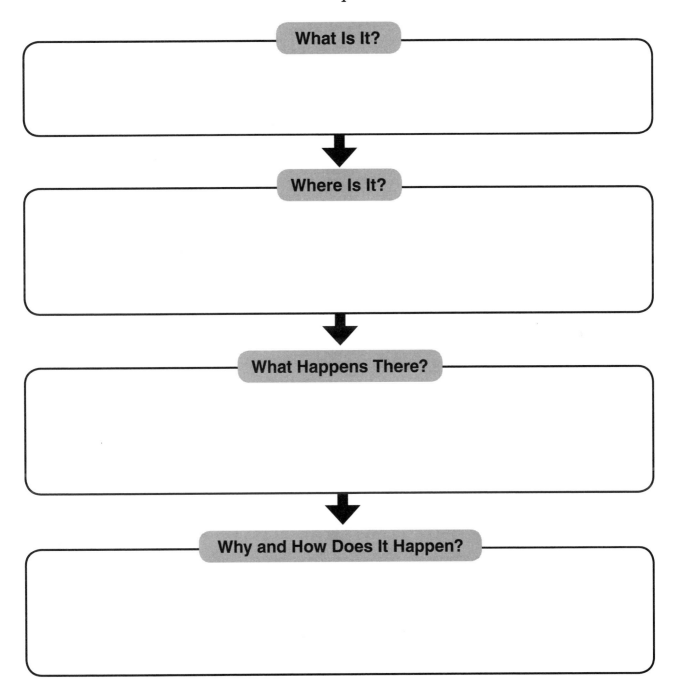

What Is It?

Where Is It?

What Happens There?

Why and How Does It Happen?

UNIT
6

California's Big Shakes

Explain

Write an explanatory essay about **what the San Andreas Fault is and how it affects the land around it.** Use information from your graphic organizer and the science article.

_____

Title

_____

_____

_____

_____

_____

_____

_____

_____

_____

_____

_____

_____

_____

Evaluate Your Writing

Read about the explanatory text structure. Then use your essay to complete the activity below.

A text that **explains** tells why, where, or how something happens. Writing to explain involves including specific details about the subject.

The reason for writing is clear.

My essay explained:

_____

I introduced the subject in this topic sentence:

_____

I provided details that support the topic.

I included these detail sentences:

1. _____

2. _____

My paragraphs have a clear focus.

My first paragraph explains that:

_____

My last paragraph includes this conclusion sentence:

_____

Benjamin Franklin

Lesson Objectives

Writing
Students use information from the biography to write an opinion essay.

Vocabulary
Students learn content vocabulary words and use those words to write about Benjamin Franklin's inventions and legacy.

Content Knowledge
Students learn about the various ways Benjamin Franklin contributed to American society and life.

Essential Understanding
Students understand that people such as Benjamin Franklin helped to create the country we live in today.

Prepare the Unit

Reproduce and distribute one copy for each student.

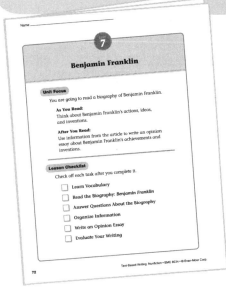

1 Unit Focus and Lesson Checklist

Distribute one unit to each student and direct students' attention to the Unit Focus and Lesson Checklist. Tell them they will be able to refer to the focus of the unit as needed while working on the lessons. Instruct students to check off each task on the checklist after they complete it.

Read aloud the focus statements, and verify that students understand their purpose for reading. Ask:

• *Who are we going to read about?* (Benjamin Franklin)

• *What are you going to learn about him?* (his actions, ideas, and inventions)

• *What are you going to write based on this biography?* (an opinion essay)

CCSS: **W** 4.1, 4.7, 4.8   **RIT** 4.3, 4.4, 4.5, 4.10

2 Learn Vocabulary

Read aloud each content vocabulary word and have students repeat. Then read aloud and discuss the definitions. Explain that students will have a better understanding of the words after they read the biography. Have students write the vocabulary words on the provided lines.

3 Read the Biography: *Benjamin Franklin*

Read aloud the biography as students follow along silently. Then have students reread the biography independently or in small groups.

4 Answer Questions About the Biography

To ensure reading comprehension, have students answer the text-dependent questions. Review the answers together.

5 Organize Information

Explain to students that they will use an idea-web graphic organizer to help them plan their essays. Guide students in using the text to complete the organizer.

6 Write an Opinion Essay

Have students complete the writing assignment independently, with a partner, or in small groups.

Remind students that an opinion essay:

- tells how you feel about something,
- tells why you feel that way, and
- includes signal words: *I feel, I think, to me, I like, I agree that; I don't like, I disagree that.*

7 Evaluate Your Writing

Explain that students will evaluate their writing to ensure that they have produced well-written essays that follow the opinion structure.

UNIT 7

Benjamin Franklin

Unit Focus

You are going to read a biography of Benjamin Franklin.

As You Read:

Think about Benjamin Franklin's actions, ideas, and inventions.

After You Read:

Use information from the article to write an opinion essay about Benjamin Franklin's achievements and inventions.

Lesson Checklist

Check off each task after you complete it.

- [ ] Learn Vocabulary
- [ ] Read the Biography: *Benjamin Franklin*
- [ ] Answer Questions About the Biography
- [ ] Organize Information
- [ ] Write an Opinion Essay
- [ ] Evaluate Your Writing

Benjamin Franklin

Learn Vocabulary

Read the word and its definition.
Then write the vocabulary word on the line.

1. **almanac**   a reference book filled with statistics about weather, sports, or specific interests   _____

2. **clever**   smart, wise, intelligent   _____

3. **inducted**   invited into a special organization or group   _____

4. **official**   someone who has been elected by the public into an office, such as the president or a sheriff   _____

5. **planks**   flat, straight pieces of wood   _____

6. **print shop**   a place that produces books, magazines, newspapers, or other printed materials   _____

7. **switching**   trading or replacing   _____

8. **tips**   useful bits of information   _____

Benjamin Franklin

Benjamin Franklin was born in 1706 in Boston, Massachusetts. He was always filled with ideas and loved to read. His family couldn't afford to keep him in school, however, so he went to work in his brother's print shop when he was 12 years old. When Franklin was 22, he set up his own print shop in Philadelphia, Pennsylvania. Beginning in 1729, he wrote and published the *Pennsylvania Gazette* newspaper. From 1732 to 1757, he printed *Poor Richard's Almanac* once a year. The almanac provided weather forecasts, household tips, and other helpful information. *Poor Richard's Almanac* was very popular because it also included stories and words of wisdom. Franklin is remembered for many well-known sayings, such as "Well done is better than well said."

From the time he was a boy, Franklin spent his time inventing things that would make life easier. When he was 11, he had an idea that would help him swim faster. He made "fins" for his hands from pieces of thin wood. The wood was cut in oval shapes and had holes for his thumbs. He also strapped wood planks to his feet, but those slowed him down. Franklin continued to love swimming throughout his lifetime. He encouraged others to exercise in water. Because of his involvement with the sport, Franklin was inducted into the International Swimming Hall of Fame in 1968, which was 178 years after his death. Franklin also created Philadelphia's first fire department and its first police department. He then went on to organize the first hospital and the first library in the United States.

As Franklin aged, he developed vision problems. Sometimes he needed to wear eyeglasses to see things that were far away. At other times, he needed glasses to help him see or read things

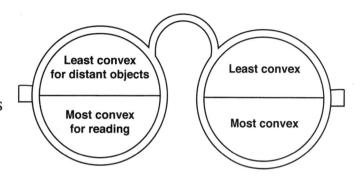

that were very close or small. Franklin used two different pairs of glasses for these issues, and he grew tired of switching between them. In a very clever move, he cut the lenses of each pair in half. He used the halves to make two new pairs of bifocal glasses. The bottom halves helped him see things nearby. The top halves helped him see things that were far away. Today, people with vision issues can wear glasses or contact lenses based on Franklin's design.

Benjamin Franklin is best known for his role in the creation of the United States. He helped write the Declaration of Independence and the U.S. Constitution, and he signed both. Franklin continued to serve as a U.S. government official for the rest of his life. When Franklin died in 1790, 20,000 people attended his funeral.

Benjamin Franklin

Answer Questions

Read and answer each question.

1. Benjamin Franklin first worked at a ____.

   Ⓐ swimming pool

   Ⓑ print shop

   Ⓒ library

2. Which of these was included in *Poor Richard's Almanac*?

   Ⓐ designs for eyeglasses

   Ⓑ newspaper articles

   Ⓒ forecasts about the weather

3. Franklin first started working at age 12 because ____.

   Ⓐ his parents couldn't afford to pay for his schooling

   Ⓑ he wanted to focus on inventing helpful items

   Ⓒ his brother needed help writing *Poor Richard's Almanac*

4. Which of the following did Franklin <u>not</u> help to create?

   Ⓐ the first library

   Ⓑ the first Philadelphia police department

   Ⓒ the International Swimming Hall of Fame

5. Why do you think Franklin was honored 178 years after his death?

   _____

   _____

   _____

6. Was Franklin respected during his lifetime? How do you know?

   _____

   _____

Organize Information

Read the biography again. Then write information in the graphic organizer that tells about Franklin's actions, ideas, and inventions. List facts from the biography.

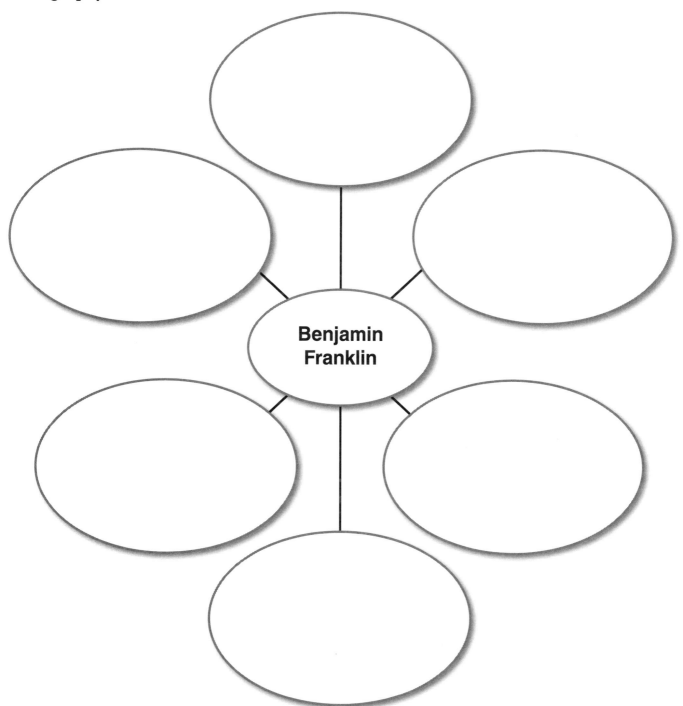

Benjamin Franklin

Benjamin Franklin

Opinion

Write an essay that tells your opinion about **Benjamin Franklin**. Are his achievements and inventions still important today? Why or why not? Use information from your graphic organizer and the biography.

_____

Title

_____

_____

_____

_____

_____

_____

_____

_____

_____

_____

_____

_____

_____

_____

Evaluate Your Writing

Read about the opinion structure. Then use your essay to complete the activity below.

A text that gives an **opinion** tells how you personally feel about a subject and why you feel that way. It also includes reasons that support your opinion.

The reason for writing is clear.

My essay explained my opinion and the reasons for my opinion about:

_____

I used these opinion signal words:

_____   _____   _____

I provided reasons that support my opinion.

I included these reasons:

1. _____

2. _____

My last paragraph has a strong conclusion.

My opening sentence for the last paragraph is:

_____

My conclusion sentence for the last paragraph is:

_____

The Biggest Bridge

Lesson Objectives

Writing
Students use information from the social studies article to write an opinion essay.

Vocabulary
Students learn content vocabulary words and use those words to write about the Akashi Kaikyo Bridge in Japan.

Content Knowledge
Students learn how and why the Akashi Kaikyo Bridge was created.

Essential Understanding
Students understand that projects like the bridge, despite the time spent or the cost, are worth it in order to save human lives.

Prepare the Unit

Reproduce and distribute one copy for each student.

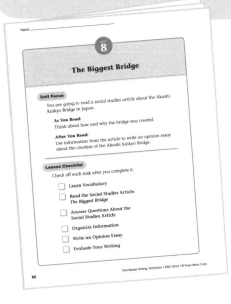

1 Unit Focus and Lesson Checklist

Distribute one unit to each student and direct students' attention to the Unit Focus and Lesson Checklist. Tell them they will be able to refer to the focus of the unit as needed while working on the lessons. Instruct students to check off each task on the checklist after they complete it.

Read aloud the focus statements, and verify that students understand their purpose for reading. Ask:

- *What are we going to read about?* (the Akashi Kaikyo Bridge)

- *What are you going to learn about it?* (how and why it was created)

- *What are you going to write based on this article?* (an opinion essay)

CCSS: **W** 4.1, 4.7, 4.8   **RIT** 4.3, 4.4, 4.5, 4.10

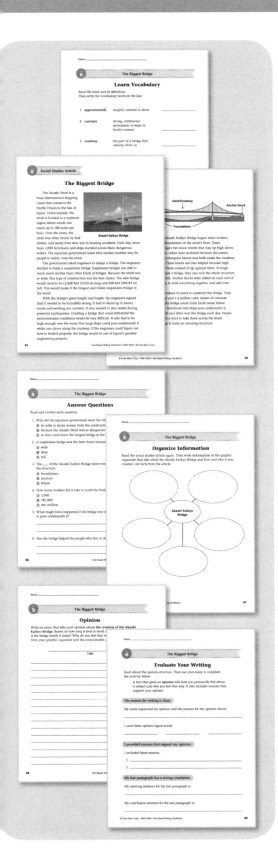

2 Learn Vocabulary

Read aloud each content vocabulary word and have students repeat. Then read aloud and discuss the definitions. Explain that students will have a better understanding of the words after they read the social studies article. Have students write the vocabulary words on the provided lines.

3 Read the Social Studies Article: *The Biggest Bridge*

Read aloud the social studies article as students follow along silently. Then have students reread the article independently or in small groups.

4 Answer Questions About the Social Studies Article

To ensure reading comprehension, have students answer the text-dependent questions. Review the answers together.

5 Organize Information

Explain to students that they will use an idea-web graphic organizer to help them plan their essays. Guide students in using the text to complete the organizer.

6 Write an Opinion Essay

Have students complete the writing assignment independently, with a partner, or in small groups.

Remind students that an opinion essay:

- tells how you feel about something,

- tells why you feel that way, and

- includes signal words: *I feel, I think, to me, I like, I agree that; I don't like, I disagree that.*

7 Evaluate Your Writing

Explain that students will evaluate their writing to ensure that they have produced well-written essays that follow the opinion structure.

UNIT
8

The Biggest Bridge

Unit Focus

You are going to read a social studies article about the Akashi Kaikyo Bridge in Japan.

As You Read:

Think about how and why the bridge was created.

After You Read:

Use information from the article to write an opinion essay about the creation of the Akashi Kaikyo Bridge.

Lesson Checklist

Check off each task after you complete it.

☐ **Learn Vocabulary**

☐ **Read the Social Studies Article:** *The Biggest Bridge*

☐ **Answer Questions About the Social Studies Article**

☐ **Organize Information**

☐ **Write an Opinion Essay**

☐ **Evaluate Your Writing**

Learn Vocabulary

Read the word and its definition.
Then write the vocabulary word on the line.

1. **approximately**   roughly; around or about   _____

2. **currents**   strong, continuous movements of water in Earth's oceans   _____

3. **roadway**   the part of a bridge that vehicles drive on   _____

4. **shipping canal**   a body of water designed to help large ships easily transport goods from one location to another   _____

5. **stable**   in balance; not moving   _____

6. **swirling**   moving in a circular pattern   _____

7. **typhoon**   a storm involving wind and water; a hurricane or cyclone   _____

8. **withstand**   to stay strong or resist the effects of; to not fail   _____

The Biggest Bridge

The Akashi Strait is a busy international shipping canal that connects the Pacific Ocean to the Sea of Japan. Unfortunately, the strait is located in a typhoon region where winds can reach up to 180 miles per hour. Over the years, the strait was often struck by bad

Akashi Kaikyo Bridge

storms, and many lives were lost in boating accidents. Each day, more than 1,000 ferryboats and ships traveled across these dangerous waters. The Japanese government knew they needed another way for people to safely cross the strait.

The government asked engineers to design a bridge. The engineers decided to build a suspension bridge. Suspension bridges are able to reach much farther than other kinds of bridges. Because the strait was so wide, this type of construction was the best choice. The new bridge would need to be 12,828 feet (3,910 m) long and 928 feet (282.85 m) tall. This would make it the longest and tallest suspension bridge in the world.

With the bridge's great length and height, the engineers agreed that it needed to be incredibly strong. It had to stand up to heavy winds and swirling sea currents. It also needed to stay stable during powerful earthquakes. Creating a bridge that could withstand the environmental conditions would be very difficult. It also had to be high enough over the water that large ships could pass underneath it while cars drove along the roadway. If the engineers could figure out how to build it properly, the bridge would be one of Japan's greatest engineering projects.

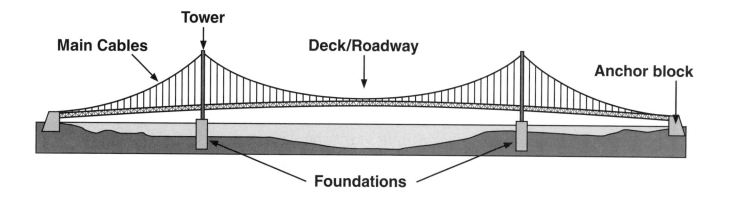

Construction of the Akashi Kaikyo Bridge began when workers installed huge concrete foundations in the strait's floor. These foundations held the bridge's two main towers that rose up high above the water. Then two main cables were stretched between the towers.

A network of special triangular braces was built under the roadway to give it extra strength. These braces are also helpful because high winds can blow through them instead of up against them. If rough winds blow directly against a bridge, they can rock the whole structure dangerously back and forth. Anchor blocks were added on each end of the Akashi Kaikyo Bridge to hold everything together and add even more support.

It took two million workers 10 years to construct the bridge. They used 181,000 tons of steel and 1.4 million cubic meters of concrete. The steel cable used for the bridge could circle Earth seven times! Today, not only do 1,000 ferryboats and ships pass underneath it, but approximately 23,000 cars drive over the bridge each day. People no longer have to wait for a ferry to take them across the strait. The Akashi Kaikyo Bridge is truly an amazing structure.

UNIT
8

The Biggest Bridge

Answer Questions

Read and answer each question.

1. Why did the Japanese government want the Akashi Kaikyo Bridge built?

   Ⓐ in order to make money from the construction

   Ⓑ because the Akashi Strait was so dangerous

   Ⓒ so they could have the longest bridge in the world

2. A suspension bridge was the best choice because the strait was so ____.

   Ⓐ wide

   Ⓑ deep

   Ⓒ tall

3. The ____ of the Akashi Kaikyo Bridge allow wind to pass through the structure.

   Ⓐ foundations

   Ⓑ anchors

   Ⓒ braces

4. How many workers did it take to build the bridge?

   Ⓐ 1,000

   Ⓑ 181,000

   Ⓒ two million

5. What might have happened if the bridge was not tall enough for ships to pass underneath it?

   _____

   _____

6. Has the bridge helped the people who live in the area? How do you know?

   _____

   _____

Name _____

Organize Information

Read the social studies article again. Then write information in the graphic organizer that tells about the Akashi Kaikyo Bridge and how and why it was created. List facts from the article.

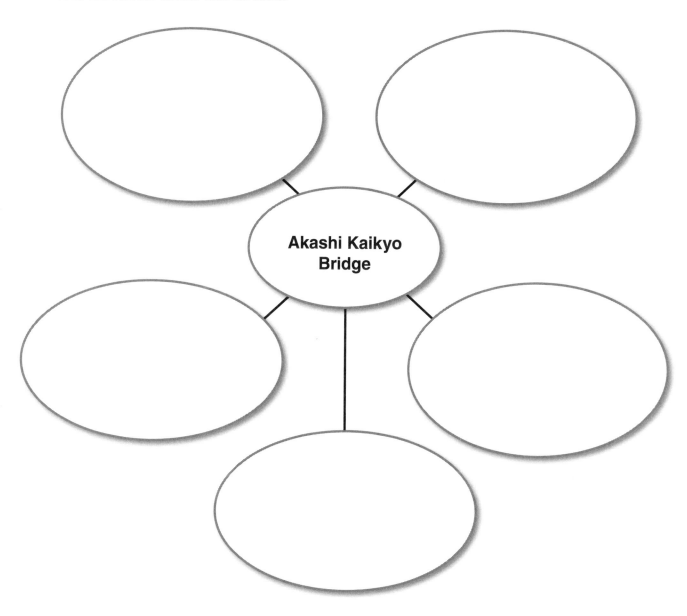

Akashi Kaikyo Bridge

Name _____

Opinion

Write an essay that tells your opinion about **the creation of the Akashi Kaikyo Bridge**. Based on how long it took to build and how much it cost, is the bridge worth it today? Why do you feel that way? Use information from your graphic organizer and the social studies article.

_____

Title

_____

_____

_____

_____

_____

_____

_____

_____

_____

_____

_____

_____

_____

_____

Evaluate Your Writing

Read about the opinion structure. Then use your essay to complete the activity below.

> A text that gives an **opinion** tells how you personally feel about a subject and why you feel that way. It also includes reasons that support your opinion.

The reason for writing is clear.

My essay explained my opinion and the reasons for my opinion about:

_____

I used these opinion signal words:

_____   _____   _____

I provided reasons that support my opinion.

I included these reasons:

1. _____

2. _____

My last paragraph has a strong conclusion.

My opening sentence for the last paragraph is:

_____

My conclusion sentence for the last paragraph is:

_____

Genetic Traits

Lesson Objectives

Writing
Students use information from the science article to write an argument essay.

Vocabulary
Students learn content vocabulary words and use those words to write about whether animals need or do not need their special genetic traits to survive.

Content Knowledge
Students learn how genes produce traits that help to protect animals in their natural habitats.

Essential Understanding
Students understand that without special traits, many animals would not be able to hunt, stay safe, or live in extreme weather conditions.

Prepare the Unit

Reproduce and distribute one copy for each student.

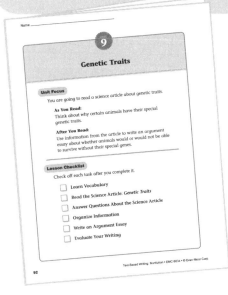

1 Unit Focus and Lesson Checklist

Distribute one unit to each student and direct students' attention to the Unit Focus and Lesson Checklist. Tell them they will be able to refer to the focus of the unit as needed while working on the lessons. Instruct students to check off each task on the checklist after they complete it.

Read aloud the focus statements, and verify that students understand their purpose for reading. Ask:

- *What are we going to read about?* (genetic traits)

- *What are you going to learn about them?* (why certain animals have certain traits)

- *What are you going to write based on this article?* (an argument essay)

CCSS: **W** 4.1, 4.7, 4.8   **RIT** 4.3, 4.4, 4.5, 4.10

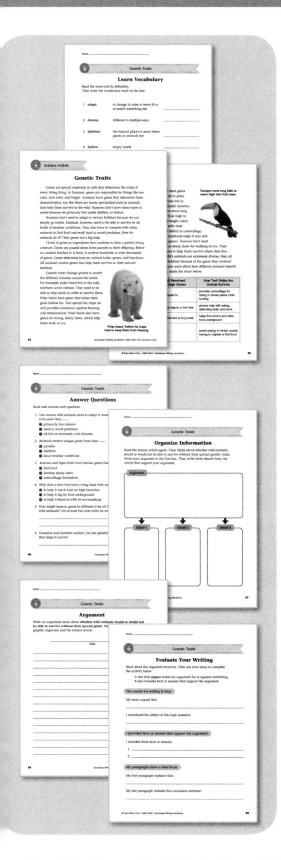

2 Learn Vocabulary

Read aloud each content vocabulary word and have students repeat. Then read aloud and discuss the definitions. Explain that students will have a better understanding of the words after they read the science article. Have students write the vocabulary words on the provided lines.

3 Read the Science Article: *Genetic Traits*

Read aloud the science article as students follow along silently. Then have students reread the article independently or in small groups.

4 Answer Questions About the Science Article

To ensure reading comprehension, have students answer the text-dependent questions. Review the answers together.

5 Organize Information

Explain to students that they will use an argument graphic organizer to help them plan their essays. Guide students in using the text to complete the organizer.

6 Write an Argument Essay

Have students complete the writing assignment independently, with a partner, or in small groups.

Remind students that an argument essay:

• makes an argument for or against something,

• gives reasons or facts to support the argument, and

• includes an introductory topic sentence and a conclusion sentence at the end.

7 Evaluate Your Writing

Explain that students will evaluate their writing to ensure that they have produced well-written essays that follow the argument structure.

UNIT
9

Genetic Traits

Unit Focus

You are going to read a science article about genetic traits.

As You Read:

Think about why certain animals have their special genetic traits.

After You Read:

Use information from the article to write an argument essay about whether animals would or would not be able to survive without their special genes.

Lesson Checklist

Check off each task after you complete it.

- [ ] **Learn Vocabulary**
- [ ] **Read the Science Article: *Genetic Traits***
- [ ] **Answer Questions About the Science Article**
- [ ] **Organize Information**
- [ ] **Write an Argument Essay**
- [ ] **Evaluate Your Writing**

Name _____

Learn Vocabulary

Read the word and its definition.
Then write the vocabulary word on the line.

1. **adapt** to change in order to better fit in or match something else _____

2. **diverse** different in multiple ways _____

3. **habitats** the natural places or areas where plants or animals live _____

4. **hollow** empty inside _____

5. **insulation** material that keeps something warm, dry, or safe from wind and weather _____

6. **predators** animals that hunt other animals for food _____

7. **specialized** unique or specific to a certain person or animal _____

8. **traits** characteristics or things that make one animal different from another animal _____

Genetic Traits

Genes are special materials in cells that determine the traits of every living thing. In humans, genes are responsible for things like eye color, hair color, and height. Animals have genes that determine these characteristics, too. But there are many specialized traits in animals that help them survive in the wild. Humans don't have these types of needs because we primarily live inside shelters, or homes.

Humans don't need to adapt to certain habitats because we can simply go inside. Animals, however, need to be able to survive in all kinds of weather conditions. They also have to compete with other animals to find food and work hard to avoid predators. How do animals do it? Their genes are a big help.

Think of genes as ingredients that combine to form a perfect living creature. Genes are passed down from parents to their offspring. Before an animal hatches or is born, it receives hundreds or even thousands of genes. Genes determine how an animal looks, grows, and functions. All animals receive genes that help them survive in their natural habitats.

Genetic traits change greatly to match the different climates around the world. For example, polar bears live in the cold, northern arctic climate. They need to be able to stay warm in order to survive there. Polar bears have genes that make them grow hollow fur. This special fur traps air and provides insulation against freezing cold temperatures. Polar bears also have genes for strong, sharp claws, which help them walk on ice.

Polar bears' hollow fur traps heat to keep them from freezing.

Other animals don't need genes exactly like the ones found in polar bears. For example, toucans live in the warm rainforests of South America. These amazing birds have extra long bills to help them reach fruit high in the trees. They also have bright colors that help them blend in with their environment. A toucan's ability to camouflage, or hide, itself within the rainforest helps it stay safe from predators such as jaguars. Toucans don't need hollow fur to stay warm or sharp claws for walking on ice. Their bodies have different genes to help them survive where they live.

Toucans have long bills to reach high into fruit trees.

Even though the world's animals are extremely diverse, they all survive in their natural habitats because of the genes they received from their parents. To learn more about how different animals benefit from their unique genes, study the chart below.

Animal	Trait Received Through Genes	How Trait Helps the Animal Survive
tiger	colorful, striped fur	provides camouflage for hiding in dense plants while hunting
crab	the ability to regrow a lost claw	pincers help with eating, defending itself, and more
kiwi bird	nostrils at the end of long beak	helps find worms and other food underground
bat that lives in cold climate	hibernation	saves energy in winter; avoids having to migrate to find food

Genetic Traits

Answer Questions

Read and answer each question.

1. One reason wild animals need to adapt to many kinds of conditions is because they ____.

   Ⓐ primarily live indoors

   Ⓑ need to avoid predators

   Ⓒ all live in extremely cold climates

2. Animals receive unique genes from their ____.

   Ⓐ parents

   Ⓑ habitats

   Ⓒ local weather conditions

3. Toucans and tigers both have similar genes that help them to ____.

   Ⓐ find food

   Ⓑ develop sharp claws

   Ⓒ camouflage themselves

4. Why does a kiwi bird have a long beak with nostrils at the end?

   Ⓐ to help it reach fruit on high branches

   Ⓑ to help it dig for food underground

   Ⓒ to help it blend in with its surroundings

5. How might human genes be different if we all had to live outside like wild animals? List at least two new traits we would need and why.

   _____

   _____

6. Visualize your favorite animal. List one genetic trait this animal has that helps it survive.

   _____

Organize Information

Read the science article again. Then think about whether wild animals would or would not be able to survive without their special genetic traits. Write your argument in the first box. Then write three details from the article that support your argument.

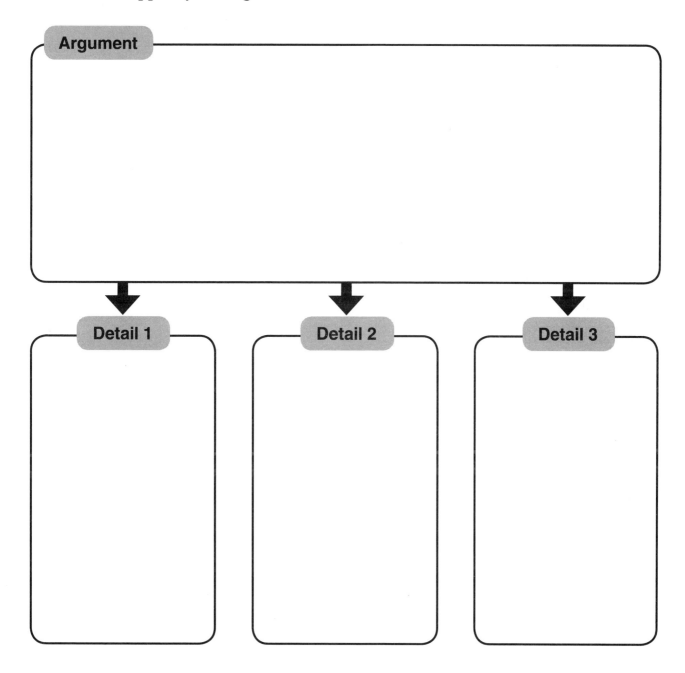

Argument

Detail 1

Detail 2

Detail 3

Argument

Write an argument essay about **whether wild animals would or would not be able to survive without their special genes.** Use information from your graphic organizer and the science article.

_____

Title

_____

_____

_____

_____

_____

_____

_____

_____

_____

_____

_____

_____

_____

UNIT 9 Genetic Traits

Evaluate Your Writing

Read about the argument structure. Then use your essay to complete the activity below.

> A text that **argues** makes an argument for or against something. It also includes facts or reasons that support the argument.

The reason for writing is clear.

My essay argued that:

_____

I introduced the subject in this topic sentence:

_____

I provided facts or reasons that support my argument.

I included these facts or reasons:

1. _____

2. _____

My paragraphs have a clear focus.

My first paragraph explains that:

_____

My last paragraph includes this conclusion sentence:

_____

Seeing with Sounds

Lesson Objectives

Writing
Students use information from the science article to write an argument essay.

Vocabulary
Students learn content vocabulary words and use those words to write about whether animals would or would not survive without echolocation.

Content Knowledge
Students learn how sounds travel and how bats and dolphins use echolocation to survive.

Essential Understanding
Students understand that bats and dolphins would have great difficulty hunting and finding their way without echolocation.

Prepare the Unit

Reproduce and distribute one copy for each student.

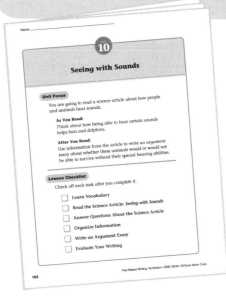

1 **Unit Focus and Lesson Checklist**

Distribute one unit to each student and direct students' attention to the Unit Focus and Lesson Checklist. Tell them they will be able to refer to the focus of the unit as needed while working on the lessons. Instruct students to check off each task on the checklist after they complete it.

Read aloud the focus statements, and verify that students understand their purpose for reading. Ask:

- *What are we going to read about?* (how people and animals hear sounds)

- *What are you going to learn about?* (how certain sounds help bats and dolphins)

- *What are you going to write based on this article?* (an argument essay)

CCSS: **W** 4.1, 4.7, 4.8   **RIT** 4.3, 4.4, 4.5, 4.10

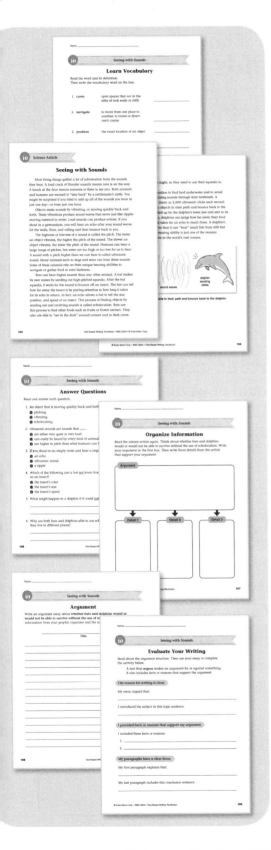

Learn Vocabulary

Read aloud each content vocabulary word and have students repeat. Then read aloud and discuss the definitions. Explain that students will have a better understanding of the words after they read the science article. Have students write the vocabulary words on the provided lines.

3 Read the Science Article: *Seeing with Sounds*

Read aloud the science article as students follow along silently. Then have students reread the article independently or in small groups.

4 Answer Questions About the Science Article

To ensure reading comprehension, have students answer the text-dependent questions. Review the answers together.

5 Organize Information

Explain to students that they will use an argument graphic organizer to help them plan their essays. Guide students in using the text to complete the organizer.

6 Write an Argument Essay

Have students complete the writing assignment independently, with a partner, or in small groups.

Remind students that an argument essay:

- makes an argument for or against something,

- gives reasons or facts to support the argument, and

- includes an introductory topic sentence and a conclusion sentence at the end.

7 Evaluate Your Writing

Explain that students will evaluate their writing to ensure that they have produced well-written essays that follow the argument structure.

UNIT 10

Seeing with Sounds

Unit Focus

You are going to read a science article about how people and animals hear sounds.

As You Read:

Think about how being able to hear certain sounds helps bats and dolphins.

After You Read:

Use information from the article to write an argument essay about whether these animals would or would not be able to survive without their special hearing abilities.

Lesson Checklist

Check off each task after you complete it.

☐ **Learn Vocabulary**

☐ **Read the Science Article: *Seeing with Sounds***

☐ **Answer Questions About the Science Article**

☐ **Organize Information**

☐ **Write an Argument Essay**

☐ **Evaluate Your Writing**

Name _____

Learn Vocabulary

Read the word and its definition.
Then write the vocabulary word on the line.

1. **caves**   open spaces that are in the
                   sides of rock walls or cliffs   _____

2. **navigate**   to move from one place to
                   another; to travel or direct
                   one's course   _____

3. **position**   the exact location of an object   _____

4. **range**   a variety or an amount
                   between certain limits   _____

5. **sensitive**   able to see, feel, or notice small
                   changes easily   _____

6. **strike**   to hit; to run into   _____

7. **thrive**   to live well; to be healthy and
                   strong   _____

8. **vibrating**   moving back and forth very
                   quickly   _____

Seeing with Sounds

Most living things gather a lot of information from the sounds they hear. A loud crack of thunder usually means rain is on the way. A knock at the door means someone is there to see you. Both animals and humans are warned to "stay back" by a rattlesnake's rattle. You might be surprised if you tried to add up all of the sounds you hear in just one day—or even just one hour.

Objects make sounds by vibrating, or moving quickly back and forth. These vibrations produce sound waves that move just like ripples moving outward in water. Loud sounds can produce echoes. If you shout in a gymnasium, you will hear an echo after your sound waves hit the walls, floor, and ceiling and then bounce back to you.

The highness or lowness of a sound is called the pitch. The faster an object vibrates, the higher the pitch of the sound. The slower an object vibrates, the lower the pitch of the sound. Humans can hear a large range of pitches, but some are too high or too low for us to hear. A sound with a pitch higher than we can hear is called ultrasonic sound. Many animals such as dogs and mice can hear these sounds. Some of these animals rely on their unique hearing abilities to navigate or gather food in total darkness.

Bats can hear higher sounds than any other animal. A bat makes its own noises by sending out high-pitched squeaks. After the bat squeaks, it waits for the sound to bounce off an insect. The bat can tell how far away the insect is by paying attention to how long it takes for its echo to return. In fact, an echo allows a bat to tell the size, position, and speed of an insect. This process of finding objects by sending out and receiving sounds is called echolocation. Bats use this process to find other foods such as fruits or flower nectars. They also are able to "see in the dark" around corners and in dark caves.

Bats come out to hunt at night, so they need to use their squeaks in order to stay healthy.

Dolphins use echolocation to find food underwater and to avoid obstacles. They make clicking sounds through their foreheads. A dolphin can send out as many as 2,000 ultrasonic clicks each second. These sound waves strike objects in their path and bounce back to the dolphin. The echo is picked up by the dolphin's lower jaw and sent to its ears and brain. Like bats, dolphins can judge how far away their food is by the length of time it takes for an echo to reach them. A dolphin's echolocation is so sensitive that it can "hear" small fish from 600 feet (182.88 m) away. This amazing ability is just one of the reasons dolphins are able to thrive in the world's vast oceans.

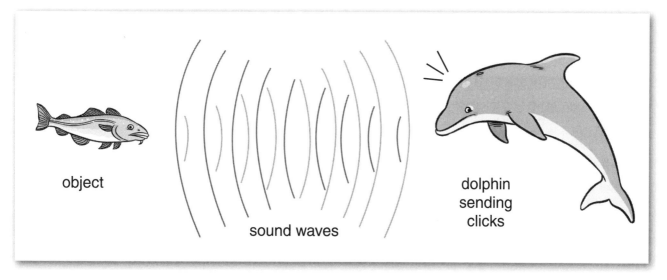

object

sound waves

dolphin sending clicks

Sound waves strike objects in their path and bounce back to the dolphin.

Answer Questions

Read and answer each question.

1. An object that is moving quickly back and forth is ____.

   Ⓐ pitching

   Ⓑ vibrating

   Ⓒ echolocating

2. Ultrasonic sounds are sounds that ____.

   Ⓐ are either very quiet or very loud

   Ⓑ can easily be heard by every kind of animal

   Ⓒ are higher in pitch than what humans can hear

3. If you shout in an empty room and hear a response, you are hearing ____.

   Ⓐ an echo

   Ⓑ ultrasonic sound

   Ⓒ a ripple

4. Which of the following can a bat <u>not</u> learn from using echolocation on an insect?

   Ⓐ the insect's color

   Ⓑ the insect's size

   Ⓒ the insect's speed

5. What might happen to a dolphin if it could <u>not</u> use echolocation?

   _____

   _____

6. Why are both bats and dolphins able to use echolocation even though they live in different places?

   _____

   _____

Organize Information

Read the science article again. Think about whether bats and dolphins would or would not be able to survive without the use of echolocation. Write your argument in the first box. Then write three details from the article that support your argument.

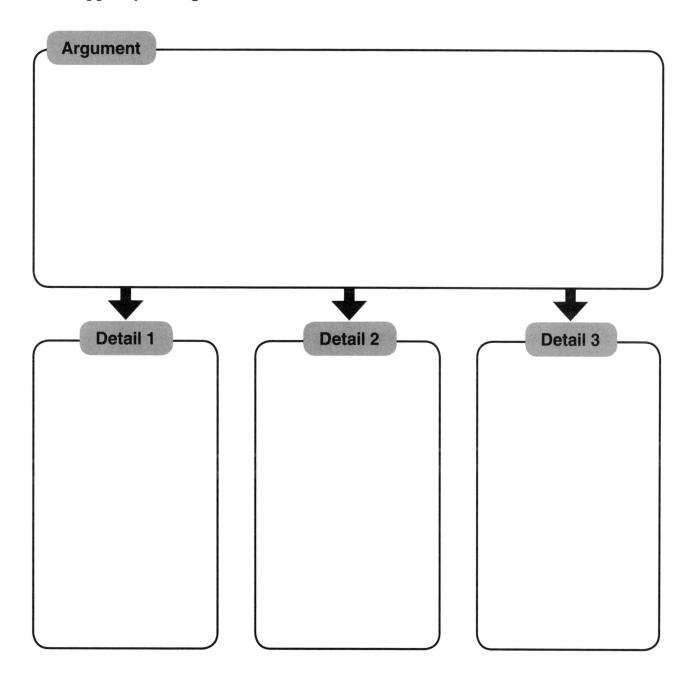

Argument

Detail 1

Detail 2

Detail 3

Name _____

Argument

Write an argument essay about **whether bats and dolphins would or would not be able to survive without the use of echolocation.** Use information from your graphic organizer and the science article.

_____

Title

_____

_____

_____

_____

_____

_____

_____

_____

_____

_____

_____

_____

Name _____

Evaluate Your Writing

Read about the argument structure. Then use your essay to complete the activity below.

> A text that **argues** makes an argument for or against something. It also includes facts or reasons that support the argument.

The reason for writing is clear.

My essay argued that:

_____

I introduced the subject in this topic sentence:

_____

I provided facts or reasons that support my argument.

I included these facts or reasons:

1. _____

2. _____

My paragraphs have a clear focus.

My first paragraph explains that:

_____

My last paragraph includes this conclusion sentence:

_____

The Study of Garbage

Lesson Objectives

Writing

Students use information from the social studies article to write an argument essay.

Vocabulary

Students learn content vocabulary words and use those words to write about whether it is or is not important to study garbage.

Content Knowledge

Students learn what people are throwing away and how they can help to control garbage levels in the future.

Essential Understanding

Students understand that we all benefit from recycling items and creating less trash.

Prepare the Unit

Reproduce and distribute one copy for each student.

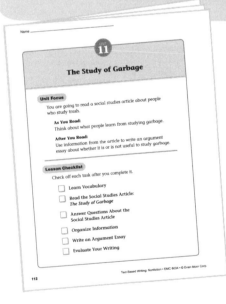

1 Unit Focus and Lesson Checklist

Distribute one unit to each student and direct students' attention to the Unit Focus and Lesson Checklist. Tell them they will be able to refer to the focus of the unit as needed while working on the lessons. Instruct students to check off each task on the checklist after they complete it.

Read aloud the focus statements, and verify that students understand their purpose for reading. Ask:

- *What are we going to read about?* (people who study trash)

- *What are you going to learn about them?* (what they learn from studying garbage)

- *What are you going to write based on this article?* (an argument essay)

CCSS: **W** 4.1, 4.7, 4.8 **RIT** 4.3, 4.4, 4.5, 4.10

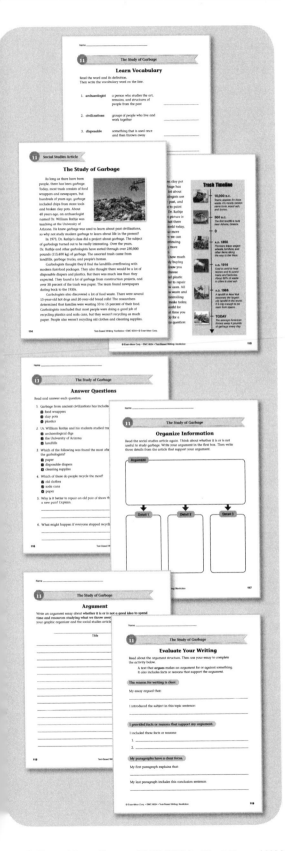

2 Learn Vocabulary

Read aloud each content vocabulary word and have students repeat. Then read aloud and discuss the definitions. Explain that students will have a better understanding of the words after they read the social studies article. Have students write the vocabulary words on the provided lines.

3 Read the Social Studies Article: *The Study of Garbage*

Read aloud the social studies article as students follow along silently. Then have students reread the article independently or in small groups.

4 Answer Questions About the Social Studies Article

To ensure reading comprehension, have students answer the text-dependent questions. Review the answers together.

5 Organize Information

Explain to students that they will use an argument graphic organizer to help them plan their essays. Guide students in using the text to complete the organizer.

6 Write an Argument Essay

Have students complete the writing assignment independently, with a partner, or in small groups.

Remind students that an argument essay:

- makes an argument for or against something,

- gives reasons or facts to support the argument, and

- includes an introductory topic sentence and a conclusion sentence at the end.

7 Evaluate Your Writing

Explain that students will evaluate their writing to ensure that they have produced well-written essays that follow the argument structure.

UNIT
11

The Study of Garbage

Unit Focus

You are going to read a social studies article about people who study trash.

As You Read:

Think about what people learn from studying garbage.

After You Read:

Use information from the article to write an argument essay about whether it is or is not useful to study garbage.

Lesson Checklist

Check off each task after you complete it.

☐ **Learn Vocabulary**

☐ **Read the Social Studies Article:** *The Study of Garbage*

☐ **Answer Questions About the Social Studies Article**

☐ **Organize Information**

☐ **Write an Argument Essay**

☐ **Evaluate Your Writing**

Learn Vocabulary

Read the word and its definition.
Then write the vocabulary word on the line.

1. **archaeologist**   a person who studies the art, remains, and structures of people from the past   _____

2. **civilizations**   groups of people who live and work together   _____

3. **disposable**   something that is used once and then thrown away   _____

4. **garbology**   the study of what people use and what they throw away   _____

5. **landfills**   large, special areas for the long-term storage of garbage   _____

6. **modern**   relating to the present time   _____

7. **recycling**   using an item multiple times or in new ways   _____

8. **stone tools**   tools made out of stone, such as hammers, knives, or scrapers   _____

The Study of Garbage

As long as there have been people, there has been garbage. Today, most trash consists of food wrappers and newspapers, but hundreds of years ago, garbage included chips from stone tools and broken clay pots. About 40 years ago, an archaeologist named Dr. William Rathje was teaching at the University of

Arizona. He knew garbage was used to learn about past civilizations, so why not study modern garbage to learn about life in the present?

In 1973, Dr. Rathje's class did a project about garbage. The subject of garbology turned out to be really interesting. Over the years, Dr. Rathje and other garbologists have sorted through over 250,000 pounds (113,400 kg) of garbage. The assorted trash came from landfills, garbage trucks, and people's homes.

Garbologists thought they'd find the landfills overflowing with modern fast-food packages. They also thought there would be a lot of disposable diapers and plastics. But there was much less than they expected. They found a lot of garbage from construction projects, and over 50 percent of the trash was paper. The team found newspapers dating back to the 1930s.

Garbologists also discovered a lot of food waste. There were several 15-year-old hot dogs and 20-year-old bread rolls! The researchers determined that families were wasting 10 to 15 percent of their food. Garbologists concluded that most people were doing a good job of recycling plastics and soda cans, but they weren't recycling as much paper. People also weren't recycling old clothes and cleaning supplies.

Whether it is a broken clay pot or a candy wrapper, garbage has helped scientists learn a lot about how people live. Archaeologists use garbage to peek into the past, and garbologists use garbage to paint a picture of the present. Dr. Rathje doesn't think our present picture is too bad. He recognizes that there are more people in the world today, which means there is also more trash. But he does believe we can make a difference by continuing to recycle and by paying more attention to what we buy.

You can help control how much garbage is created by only buying the amount of food you *know* you will eat. It also helps to choose things with less paper and plastic packaging. And it is better to repair old items than to buy new ones. All of these actions make less waste and use fewer resources. By controlling how much garbage you make today, you can create a better world for people in the future. Next time you take out the garbage, stop for a moment. Ask yourself this question: *Is this **really** garbage?*

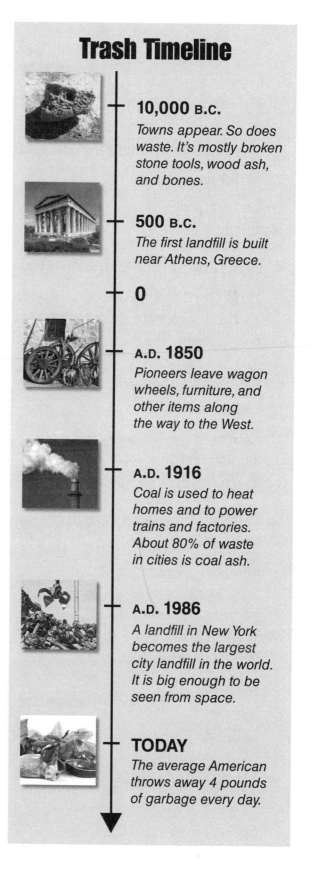

Trash Timeline

10,000 B.C.
Towns appear. So does waste. It's mostly broken stone tools, wood ash, and bones.

500 B.C.
The first landfill is built near Athens, Greece.

0

A.D. 1850
Pioneers leave wagon wheels, furniture, and other items along the way to the West.

A.D. 1916
Coal is used to heat homes and to power trains and factories. About 80% of waste in cities is coal ash.

A.D. 1986
A landfill in New York becomes the largest city landfill in the world. It is big enough to be seen from space.

TODAY
The average American throws away 4 pounds of garbage every day.

The Study of Garbage

Answer Questions

Read and answer each question.

1. Garbage from ancient civilizations has included ____.

   Ⓐ food wrappers

   Ⓑ clay pots

   Ⓒ plastics

2. Dr. William Rathje and his students studied trash found in ____.

   Ⓐ archaeological digs

   Ⓑ the University of Arizona

   Ⓒ landfills

3. Which of the following was found the most often by Dr. Rathje and the garbologists?

   Ⓐ paper

   Ⓑ disposable diapers

   Ⓒ cleaning supplies

4. Which of these do people recycle the most?

   Ⓐ old clothes

   Ⓑ soda cans

   Ⓒ paper

5. Why is it better to repair an old pair of shoes than it is to buy a new pair? Explain.

   _____

   _____

6. What might happen if everyone stopped recycling today?

   _____

   _____

Name _____

Organize Information

Read the social studies article again. Think about whether it is or is not useful to study garbage. Write your argument in the first box. Then write three details from the article that support your argument.

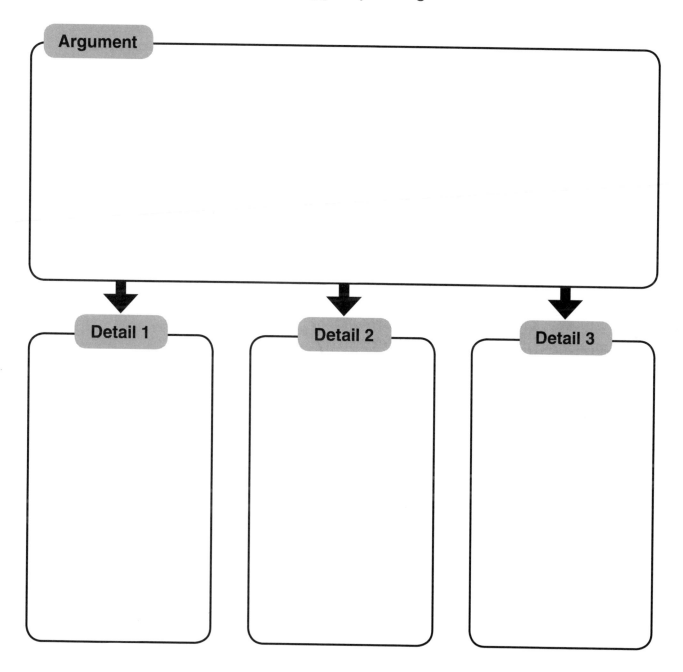

Argument

Detail 1

Detail 2

Detail 3

Name _____

Argument

Write an argument essay about **whether it is or is not a good idea to spend time and resources studying what we throw away.** Use information from your graphic organizer and the social studies article.

_____

Title

_____

_____

_____

_____

_____

_____

_____

_____

_____

_____

_____

_____

_____

UNIT
11

Evaluate Your Writing

Read about the argument structure. Then use your essay to complete the activity below.

> A text that **argues** makes an argument for or against something. It also includes facts or reasons that support the argument.

The reason for writing is clear.

My essay argued that:

_____

I introduced the subject in this topic sentence:

_____

I provided facts or reasons that support my argument.

I included these facts or reasons:

1. _____

2. _____

My paragraphs have a clear focus.

My first paragraph explains that:

_____

My last paragraph includes this conclusion sentence:

_____

McDonald Observatory

Lesson Objectives

Writing
Students use information from the science article to write an argument.

Vocabulary
Students learn content vocabulary words and use those words to write about whether scientists and researchers do or do not need access to large telescopes.

Content Knowledge
Students learn about the McDonald Observatory telescopes and how they benefit researchers and scientists.

Essential Understanding
Students understand that tools such as these telescopes help us learn more about ourselves and our universe.

Prepare the Unit

Reproduce and distribute one copy for each student.

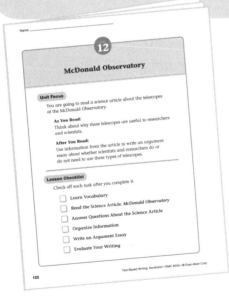

1 Unit Focus and Lesson Checklist

Distribute one unit to each student and direct students' attention to the Unit Focus and Lesson Checklist. Tell them they will be able to refer to the focus of the unit as needed while working on the lessons. Instruct students to check off each task on the checklist after they complete it.

Read aloud the focus statements, and verify that students understand their purpose for reading. Ask:

- *What are we going to read about?* (the McDonald Observatory telescopes)

- *What are you going to learn about them?* (why they are useful to researchers and scientists)

- *What are you going to write based on this article?* (an argument essay)

CCSS: **W** 4.1, 4.7, 4.8 **RIT** 4.3, 4.4, 4.5, 4.10

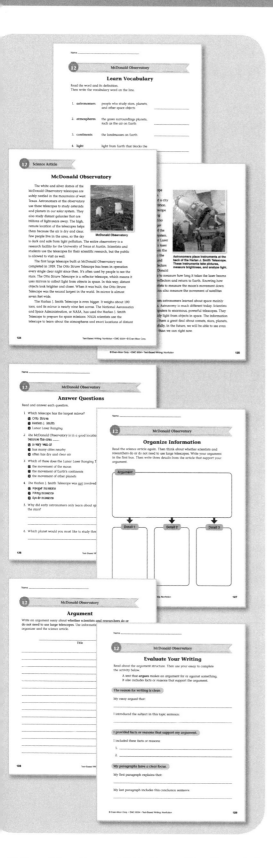

2 Learn Vocabulary

Read aloud each content vocabulary word and have students repeat. Then read aloud and discuss the definitions. Explain that students will have a better understanding of the words after they read the science article. Have students write the vocabulary words on the provided lines.

3 Read the Science Article: *McDonald Observatory*

Read aloud the science article as students follow along silently. Then have students reread the article independently or in small groups.

4 Answer Questions About the Science Article

To ensure reading comprehension, have students answer the text-dependent questions. Review the answers together.

5 Organize Information

Explain to students that they will use an argument graphic organizer to help them plan their essays. Guide students in using the text to complete the organizer.

6 Write an Argument Essay

Have students complete the writing assignment independently, with a partner, or in small groups.

Remind students that an argument essay:

- makes an argument for or against something,

- gives reasons or facts to support the argument, and

- includes an introductory topic sentence and a conclusion sentence at the end.

7 Evaluate Your Writing

Explain that students will evaluate their writing to ensure that they have produced well-written essays that follow the argument structure.

UNIT
12

McDonald Observatory

Unit Focus

You are going to read a science article about the telescopes at the McDonald Observatory.

As You Read:

Think about why these telescopes are useful to researchers and scientists.

After You Read:

Use information from the article to write an argument essay about whether scientists and researchers do or do not need to use these types of telescopes.

Lesson Checklist

Check off each task after you complete it.

- [ ] **Learn Vocabulary**
- [ ] **Read the Science Article:** *McDonald Observatory*
- [ ] **Answer Questions About the Science Article**
- [ ] **Organize Information**
- [ ] **Write an Argument Essay**
- [ ] **Evaluate Your Writing**

Learn Vocabulary

Read the word and its definition.
Then write the vocabulary word on the line.

1. **astronomers**   people who study stars, planets, and other space objects   _____

2. **atmospheres**   the gases surroundings planets, such as the air on Earth   _____

3. **continents**   the landmasses on Earth   _____

4. **light pollution**   light from Earth that blocks the natural view of the stars   _____

5. **light-years**   units of measurement that tell how far light would travel through space in one year   _____

6. **observatory**   a place where people observe or study objects or natural events in space   _____

7. **operation**   in working condition or functioning   _____

8. **satellites**   machines in orbit around Earth   _____

McDonald Observatory

The white and silver domes of the McDonald Observatory telescopes are safely nestled in the mountains of west Texas. Astronomers at the observatory use these telescopes to study asteroids and planets in our solar system. They also study distant galaxies that are billions of light-years away. The high, remote location of the telescopes helps them because the air is dry and clear. Few people live in the area, so the sky is dark and safe from light pollution. The entire observatory is a research facility for the University of Texas at Austin. Scientists and students use the telescopes for their scientific research, but the public is allowed to visit as well.

McDonald Observatory

The first large telescope built at McDonald Observatory was completed in 1939. The Otto Struve Telescope has been in operation every single clear night since then. It's often used by people to see the stars. The Otto Struve Telescope is a reflector telescope, which means it uses mirrors to collect light from objects in space. In this way, distant objects look brighter and closer. When it was built, the Otto Struve Telescope was the second largest in the world. Its mirror is almost seven feet wide.

The Harlan J. Smith Telescope is even bigger. It weighs about 190 tons, and its mirror is nearly nine feet across. The National Aeronautics and Space Administration, or NASA, has used the Harlan J. Smith Telescope to prepare for space missions. NASA scientists use the telescope to learn about the atmospheres and exact locations of distant planets. Using the telescope is very similar to using a guidebook to learn about a city before you visit it on vacation. The Harlan J. Smith Telescope was used before the *Viking* mission to Mars. It was also used to prepare for *Voyager* missions, which explored the outer parts of our solar system.

Astronomers place instruments at the back of the Harlan J. Smith Telescope. These instruments take pictures, measure brightness, and analyze light.

The McDonald Lunar Laser Ranging Telescope shoots laser beams at the moon. When the *Apollo* astronauts went to the moon in the late 1960s and early 1970s, they left reflectors there. Researchers at McDonald use the 30-inch telescope to measure how long it takes the laser beams to bounce off the moon reflectors and return to Earth. Knowing how long it takes allows scientists to measure the moon's movement down to the centimeter. They can also measure the movement of satellites and Earth's continents.

There was a time when astronomers learned about space mainly by gazing up at the stars. Astronomy is much different today. Scientists attach cameras and computers to enormous, powerful telescopes. They use special devices to study light from objects in space. The information the scientists gather tells them a great deal about comets, stars, planets, and even galaxies. Hopefully, in the future, we will be able to see even farther into the universe than we can right now.

McDonald Observatory

Answer Questions

Read and answer each question.

1. Which telescope has the largest mirror?

   Ⓐ Otto Struve

   Ⓑ Harlan J. Smith

   Ⓒ Lunar Laser Ranging

2. The McDonald Observatory is in a good location for the telescopes because the area ____.

   Ⓐ is very well-lit

   Ⓑ has many cities nearby

   Ⓒ often has dry and clear air

3. Which of these does the Lunar Laser Ranging Telescope <u>not</u> measure?

   Ⓐ the movement of the moon

   Ⓑ the movement of Earth's continents

   Ⓒ the movement of other planets

4. The Harlan J. Smith Telescope was <u>not</u> involved with the ____.

   Ⓐ *Voyager* missions

   Ⓑ *Viking* missions

   Ⓒ *Apollo* missions

5. Why did early astronomers only learn about space from gazing at the stars?

   _____

   _____

6. Which planet would you most like to study through a telescope? Why?

   _____

Text-Based Writing: Nonfiction • EMC 6034 • © Evan-Moor Corp.

Organize Information

Read the science article again. Then think about whether scientists and researchers do or do not need to use large telescopes. Write your argument in the first box. Then write three details from the article that support your argument.

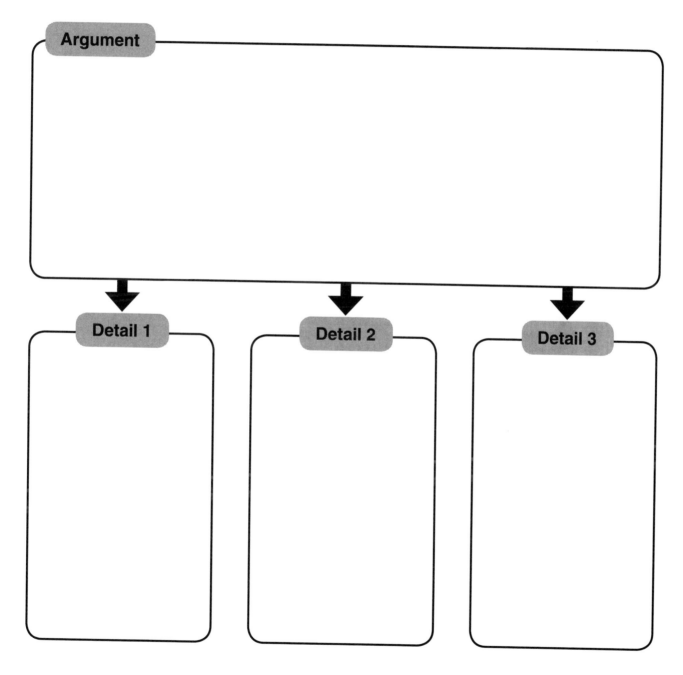

Argument

Detail 1

Detail 2

Detail 3

Name _____

Argument

Write an argument essay about **whether scientists and researchers do or do not need to use large telescopes.** Use information from your graphic organizer and the science article.

_____

Title

_____

_____

_____

_____

_____

_____

_____

_____

_____

_____

_____

_____

_____

Name _____

Evaluate Your Writing

Read about the argument structure. Then use your essay to complete the activity below.

> A text that **argues** makes an argument for or against something. It also includes facts or reasons that support the argument.

The reason for writing is clear.

My essay argued that:

_____

I introduced the subject in this topic sentence:

_____

I provided facts or reasons that support my argument.

I included these facts or reasons:

1. _____

2. _____

My paragraphs have a clear focus.

My first paragraph explains that:

_____

My last paragraph includes this conclusion sentence:

_____

Answer Key

Unit 1

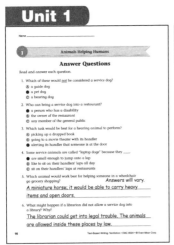

TE Page 16 / SB Page 8

TE Page 17 / SB Page 9

Unit 2

TE Page 26 / SB Page 16

TE Page 27 / SB Page 17

Unit 3

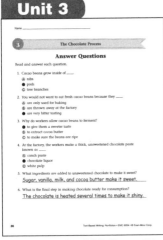

TE Page 36 / SB Page 24

TE Page 37 / SB Page 25

Unit 4

TE Page 46 / SB Page 32

TE Page 47 / SB Page 33

Unit 5

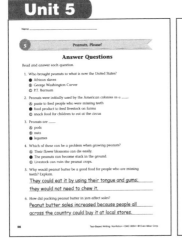

TE Page 56 / SB Page 40

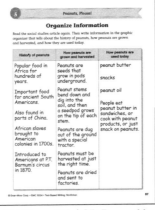

TE Page 57 / SB Page 41

Unit 6

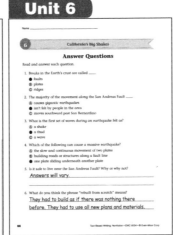

TE Page 66 / SB Page 48

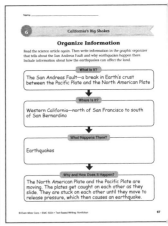

TE Page 67 / SB Page 49

Unit 7

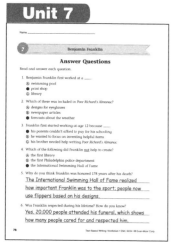

TE Page 76 / SB Page 56

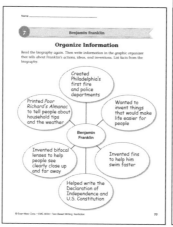

TE Page 77 / SB Page 57

Unit 8

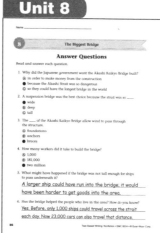

TE Page 86 / SB Page 64

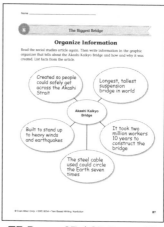

TE Page 87 / SB Page 65

Unit 9

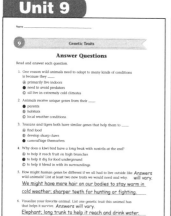

TE Page 96 / SB Page 72

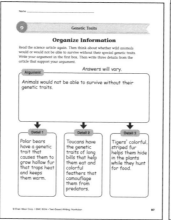

TE Page 97 / SB Page 73

Unit 10

TE Page 106 / SB Page 80

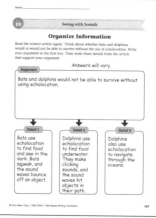

TE Page 107 / SB Page 81

Unit 11

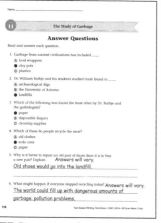

TE Page 116 / SB Page 88

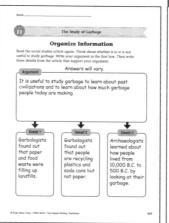

TE Page 117 / SB Page 89

Unit 12

TE Page 126 / SB Page 96

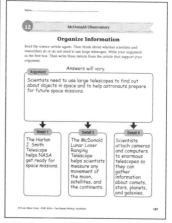

TE Page 127 / SB Page 97

Common Core Lessons

Reading Informational Text

Grade **4**

SAMPLER

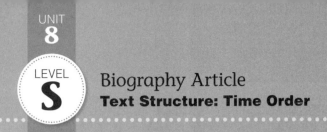

Biography Article
Text Structure: Time Order

Roald Dahl: Master Storyteller

Lesson Objective   Students will explain who Roald Dahl was and what he did during his life.

Content Knowledge   Art, writings, music, and artifacts reflect culture.

Lesson Preparation

Reproduce and distribute one copy of the article, dictionary page, and activity pages to each student.

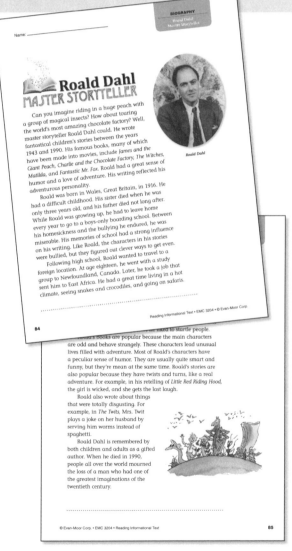

CCSS: **RIT** 4.1, 4.2, 4.3, 4.4, 4.5, 4.7   **W** 4.2, 4.4, 4.9.b

1 Read Aloud the Article

Read aloud *Roald Dahl: Master Storyteller*. Have students follow along silently as you read.

2 Introduce the Vocabulary

Content Vocabulary

Read aloud the Content Vocabulary words and definitions. Point out that *genre* is a borrowed word that comes from the French language and means "kind" or "sort." Discuss definitions and usage as needed.

Academic Vocabulary

Next, read aloud the Academic Vocabulary words and definitions. Discuss definitions and usage as needed. Then read these context sentences from the article, emphasizing the Academic Vocabulary words:

*Between his homesickness and the bullying he **endured**, he was miserable.*

*His memories of school had a strong **influence** on his writing.*

*Over the next several **decades**, Roald published other children's stories that were even more popular than the first one.*

*When he died in 1990, people all over the world **mourned** the loss of a man who had one of the greatest imaginations of the twentieth century.*

3 Students Read the Article

Have students read the article independently, with a partner, or in small groups. After students read, guide a discussion about the article. Direct students' attention to graphic elements or visual aids.

4 Identify Information

Explain that students will locate important information in the article. After students complete the activity, allow time for a question-and-answer session.

5 Answer Questions

Encourage students to use the article to answer the questions and/or check their answers.

6 Apply Vocabulary

Have students reread the article before they complete the vocabulary activity.

7 Examine Text Structure

Read aloud the Time Order description and Signal Words. Then have students read the article again, underlining signal words in red. Then guide students in completing the activity.

8 Write About It:
Roald Dahl's Life and Accomplishments

Have students complete the writing activity independently or in small groups.

Roald Dahl
MASTER STORYTELLER

Roald Dahl

Can you imagine riding in a huge peach with a group of magical insects? How about touring the world's most amazing chocolate factory? Well, master storyteller Roald Dahl could. He wrote fantastical children's stories between the years 1943 and 1990. His famous books, many of which have been made into movies, include *James and the Giant Peach, Charlie and the Chocolate Factory, The Witches, Matilda,* and *Fantastic Mr. Fox.* Roald had a great sense of humor and a love of adventure. His writing reflected his adventurous personality.

Roald was born in Wales, Great Britain, in 1916. He had a difficult childhood. His sister died when he was only three years old, and his father died not long after. While Roald was growing up, he had to leave home every year to go to a boys-only boarding school. Between his homesickness and the bullying he endured, he was miserable. His memories of school had a strong influence on his writing. Like Roald, the characters in his stories were bullied, but they figured out clever ways to get even.

Following high school, Roald wanted to travel to a foreign location. At age eighteen, he went with a study group to Newfoundland, Canada. Later, he took a job that sent him to East Africa. He had a great time living in a hot climate, seeing snakes and crocodiles, and going on safaris.

While Roald was working in Africa, World War II began. He joined the Royal Air Force, completed flight training, and flew many missions. After many adventures and several injuries, Roald moved to Washington, D.C., where he started to write short stories. His first children's book, *The Gremlins,* was published in 1943.

Over the next several decades, Roald published other children's stories that were even more popular than the first one. He also wrote stories for adults. Many of his adult stories were in the horror genre because he liked to startle people.

Roald's books are popular because the main characters are odd and behave strangely. These characters lead unusual lives filled with adventure. Most of Roald's characters have a peculiar sense of humor. They are usually quite smart and funny, but they're mean at the same time. Roald's stories are also popular because they have twists and turns, like a real adventure. For example, in his retelling of *Little Red Riding Hood,* the girl is wicked, and she gets the last laugh.

Roald also wrote about things that were totally disgusting. For example, in *The Twits,* Mrs. Twit plays a joke on her husband by serving him worms instead of spaghetti.

Roald Dahl is remembered by both children and adults as a gifted author. When he died in 1990, people all over the world mourned the loss of a man who had one of the greatest imaginations of the twentieth century.

Dictionary

Content Vocabulary

boarding school
a school where students live during the school year

fantastical
based on highly original and imaginative fantasy

genre
a specific category or type of writing, music, or art

retelling
a new version of a story

safaris
journeys to see or hunt wild animals, especially in East Africa

Academic Vocabulary

endured
lived through or put up with a difficult situation

influence
effect; the power to cause a change

decades
periods of ten years each

mourned
felt very sad, especially about a death or other loss

Write a sentence that includes at least one vocabulary word.

_____

_____

Name: _____

Identify Information

Check the box after you complete each task.

Completed

[ ]	Put brackets around important dates in the article, including when Roald Dahl was born.	☐
✎	Highlight the names of books or stories written by Roald that are mentioned in the article.	☐
☐	Draw a box around each difficulty that Roald encountered as a child.	☐
★	Put a star by the lines that tell what Roald did in Africa.	☐
~	Draw a squiggly line under sentences that name other places where Roald lived.	☐
—	Underline the sentence that tells what Roald did when World War II started.	☐
○	Circle the reason that Roald wrote horror stories for adults.	☐
✔	Put a check mark next to words and phrases that describe the characters in Roald's stories.	☐
!	Put an exclamation point next to sentences that describe why Roald Dahl's books are popular.	☐
?	Put a question mark beside any words or sentences you don't understand.	☐

Name: _____

Answer Questions

....

Use information from the article to answer each question.

1. Roald Dahl was born in _____.
   - Ⓐ East Africa
   - Ⓑ Great Britain
   - Ⓒ Canada
   - Ⓓ Washington, D.C.

2. Roald's children's books do <u>not</u> include _____.
   - Ⓐ *James and the Giant Peach*
   - Ⓑ *The Gremlins*
   - Ⓒ *Where the Wild Things Are*
   - Ⓓ *Charlie and the Chocolate Factory*

3. The best description of Roald Dahl is _____.
   - Ⓐ a struggling children's writer
   - Ⓑ a sad, lonely man
   - Ⓒ a very imaginative children's writer
   - Ⓓ a cruel, wicked man

4. What challenges did Roald face during his childhood?

   _____

   _____

5. How did Roald express his love of adventure in his books?

   _____

   _____

Name: _____

Apply Vocabulary

Use a word from the word box to complete each sentence.

Word Box

decades	genre	mourned
endured	safaris	boarding school
retelling	influence	fantastical

1. Fairy tale and science fiction are each a _____ of writing.

2. Roald Dahl _____ bullying as a child.

3. If you attend a _____, you sleep there instead of going home at night.

4. Roald's mother _____ the deaths of her husband and daughter.

5. Roald's adventurous personality had a strong _____ on his writing.

6. A _____ of a children's story might change the personalities of the characters.

7. If you go on _____ in East Africa, you're likely to see elephants, lions, and giraffes.

8. Roald wrote children's stories for more than four _____.

9. In one of Roald's _____ stories, a girl named Matilda uses her mind to move things.

Time Order

A text that has a **time order** structure presents the main idea and details in the order in which they happen.

Authors use these signal words to create a **time order** structure:

Signal Words

at	last	while	finally
next	first	later	following
when	after	before	

1. What did Roald Dahl endure in his life before finishing high school?

_____

_____

2. What is one important event that happened in Roald's life after he left East Africa?

_____

3. Write two sentences from the article that use **time order** signal words.

a. _____

_____

b. _____

_____

4. What is the final major idea mentioned in the article? Why is it mentioned last?

_____

_____

Write About It

Write a letter to your teacher about Roald Dahl. Explain who he was and what he did during his life. Include details from the article in your letter.

Roald Dahl's Life and Accomplishments

_____

_____

_____

_____

_____

_____

_____

_____

_____

_____

_____

_____

_____

_____

_____

_____

_____

_____

_____

_____